THE SUPER COOL SCIENCE OF
HARRY POTTER

The Spell-Binding Science Behind the Magic, Creatures, Witches, and Wizards of the Potter Universe!

MARK BRAKE

coauthor of *The Science of Harry Potter* and
author of *The Super Cool Science of Star Wars*

Sky Pony Press
New York

Sky Pony Press books may be purchased in bulk at special discounts for sales promotion, corporate gifts, fund-raising, or educational purposes. Special editions can also be created to specifications. For details, contact the Special Sales Department, Sky Pony Press, 307 West 36th Street, 11th Floor, New York, NY 10018 or info@skyhorsepublishing.com.

Sky Pony® is a registered trademark of Skyhorse Publishing, Inc.®, a Delaware corporation.

Visit our website at www.skyponypress.com.

10 9 8 7 6 5 4 3 2 1

Library of Congress Cataloging-in-Publication Data is available on file.

Cover design by Daniel Brount
Cover photos by gettyimages

Print ISBN: 978-1-5107-5380-8
Ebook ISBN: 978-1-5107-5381-5

Printed in China

TABLE OF CONTENTS

Part III: Herbology, Zoology, and Potions

Part IV: Magical Melting Pot

PART I

MAGICAL PHILOSOPHY

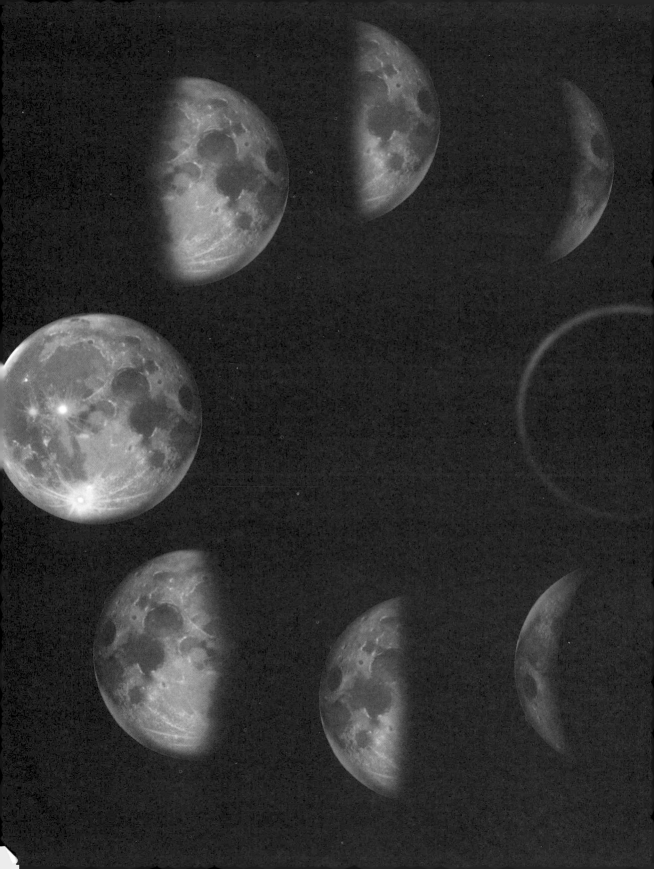

WHY DO WIZARDS AND WITCHES STUDY ASTRONOMY AT HOGWARTS?

Astronomy is the study of things in the sky. The moon, the stars, and the galaxies—the kind of stuff you can best spy through a telescope. The sun is studied in astronomy, too, but you should never look at the sun through a telescope.

But you don't even need a telescope to spy astronomy in the Harry Potter stories. Remember the wizardy werewolf Remus Lupin in *Harry Potter and the Prisoner of Azkaban*? Lupin was also known as Moony. And for good reason. Because when it was full, light from the moon was the spark that changed Remus from half-blood wizard into full-blooded werewolf!

Then there's the Enchanted Ceiling of the Great Hall at Hogwarts. The secret of this magical ceiling was that it could conjure up images of what the night sky looked like above the Hogwarts rooftops. It did this while the roof was still safe and secure above the heads of the pupils! So, instead of boring ceiling, the pupils got to see zoomed-in images of star clouds and swirling galaxies instead.

And who could forget the Astronomy Tower? It was the tallest tower at Hogwarts Castle, and the setting for one of the most dramatic ever scenes. Under the gathering darkness of the Death Eaters' Dark Mark, lurking high above the Tower, Dumbledore met his end as the result of a Killing Curse, cast by Severus Snape.

The Astronomy Tower was also where the wizards and witches studied the night sky. At midnight, under their astronomy teacher Professor Aurora Sinistra, they gazed at the planets and stars through their telescopes. But why do wizards and witches study astronomy at Hogwarts?

Planets, Stars, and Moons: Watch Out for That Werewolf!

Any witch or wizard worth their salt needs to be wary of werewolves, no matter where in the world they are. And since werewolves change during a full moon, it would be wise to know when the moon is full, and when it's going to be full! In other words, they need to know all about the moon's phases.

Besides the sun, the moon is the brightest object in the sky. The moon is silvery and bright, and if you are lucky enough to live somewhere with clear skies, you can watch the moon change, night after night. You'll see that it moves every day and that its shape is always changing. The changes in shape are what's known as the phases of the moon.

They happen because the moon is a giant ball of rock hanging in space. The moon doesn't give off its own light. Its surface is actually pretty dark, about the same darkness as a chalkboard in school. But it looks bright because it's sitting in sunlight. The sun shines on the moon, and the moon reflects that light down to earth.

So, because the moon is a ball of rock, orbiting the Earth, the way we see it lit by the sun changes with time. That's what causes the phases of the moon. The phase of the moon actually means the shape the moon appears to us as a result of how much of it we see illuminated from the earth. For example, if you see half of the moon lit and the other half dark, we say the moon is half full. When that happens, we're halfway through the month to a full moon and werewolf time! (It's no accident that the words "month" and "moon" are similar, by the way.)

Wizards and witches would know about the planets, stars, and moons, too. The names of the celestial bodies are hidden in the very names of the days of the wizarding week. In Latin, they run Sunday to Saturday, Solis (Sun/Sunday), Lunae (Moon/Monday), Martis (Mars/Tuesday), Mercurii (Mercury/Wednesday), Iovis (Jupiter/Thursday), Veneris (Venus/Friday), and Saturni (Saturn/Saturday). As you can see, even in English you can tell some days are named after celestial bodies: Sunday, Monday, and Saturday still bear the mark of sun, moon, and Saturn respectively.

If you follow the stories closely, you will also see that Hogwarts expects its students to learn and understand the movements of the planets. In one scene Hermione tells Harry he's wrong in his ideas about Europa, one of the moons of the planet Jupiter: "I think you must have misheard Professor Sinistra. Europa's covered in ice, not mice." In fact, Jupiter appears in a number of the stories. In *Harry Potter and the Sorcerer's Stone* there's a scene where Hermione is testing a reluctant Ron on astronomy. Harry meanwhile pulls a map of Jupiter toward him and begins to learn the names of its moons. And in *Harry Potter and the Order of the Phoenix*, all three of the students are having to write a tricky essay on Jupiter's moons.

A History of Astronomy and Magic

The history of astronomy, like that of magic, is a long one. And for much of that history, Muggles argued about the movements of the planets. Muggle astronomers were trying to come to grips with the way the world worked and how the sun, moon, and stars rose in our sky and then set again—that kind of thing.

One of the main ideas was that our earth was at the center of the whole universe. (The "universe" is everything that exists, the whole of space and time, and all the matter and energy within it.) In this earth-centered idea, the planets all moved in circles around the earth. This earth-centered idea also seemed to explain the movements of the sun, and the way it made its  yearly path across the sky. The idea also explained the motion of the moon. But the idea of the earth being at the center didn't explain the way in which the wandering planets moved across the sky, night after night. From the ancient days, humans had been able to see the planets Mercury, Venus, Mars, Jupiter, and Saturn with their naked eyes, which means without the use of a telescope—that hadn't been invented yet. And there was a mystery about the movements of the planets. Mercury and Venus always rose and set with the sun, either in early morning or early evening. But the planets Mars, Jupiter, and Saturn could be seen at any time of night. Why was that?

So, some daring astronomers came up with a new idea and a new system. What if, they asked, it wasn't the earth at the center, but the sun? What if the earth was also a moving planet, just like the other five? (The rest of the solar system hadn't yet been discovered.) And, guess what? The new sun-centered system worked. For the first time, astronomers figured out the correct order of the planets from the sun: Mercury, Venus, Earth, Mars, Jupiter, and Saturn. And the mystery of the movements of the planets was explained, too. Mercury and Venus always rose and set with the sun because they were inside the earth's orbit. Mars, Jupiter, and Saturn could be seen at any time of night because they were outside the earth's orbit.

The World Turned Upside Down

Then came Galileo. Galileo lived around four hundred years ago. Starting in the year 1610, he made some revolutionary discoveries about the sky, using the newly invented telescope. He found mountains and craters on the moon. He found spots on the sun. And he found thousands of stars, just like those that decorate Dumbledore's cloak. All this Galileo spied through the telescope—and a new universe was discovered.

Galileo's most amazing discovery was the main four moons of Jupiter. This was amazing because Galileo became the first person to see objects in space in orbit around something other than the earth. It showed the old earth-centered idea was wrong. The universe wasn't in orbit around the earth, after all. And Galileo's amazing discovery led to the Muggles' revolution in science, which we still see today.

So, that's another reason why wizards and witches study astronomy and the movements of the planets. They're also studying a history of Galileo's discovery of new worlds and the start of modern Muggle science!

CAN NATURE, LIKE MAGIC, CONJURE SOMETHING OUT OF NOTHING?

There are a lot of examples of conjuring in the Harry Potter stories. In *Harry Potter and the Sorcerer's Stone*, for example, Professor Quirrell snaps his fingers, and ropes spring out of thin air and wrap themselves around Harry. That's conjuring, the skill that wizards and witches have to make objects appear from "thin air."

See if you can spot these conjures that also occur in the Harry Potter stories. First, there was the case of the three brothers who conjured a bridge to get across a river. Second, a professor conjured a tea tray when he fancied a quick cuppa. And thirdly, a young lady who kept on conjuring a flock of canaries to keep herself company and conjured a crystal flask to hold another professor's memory.

Transfiguration is the branch of magic whose aim was to change the way an object looked. But Conjuration is the skill of transfiguring an object from the very air itself. This made Conjuration some of the most complex magic taught at Hogwarts. And that's why it was mostly taught to students in year six at the school.

But wizards and witches couldn't just go and conjure up any old thing out of thin air. There were limits to what could be conjured. In the stories, J. K. Rowling mentions Gamp's Law of Elemental Transfiguration. This law from the world of magic said there were some things that simply couldn't be conjured out of nothing. One of those was food. But birds and snakes, on the other hand, were a piece of cake. More than any other category of creature, birds and snakes were easiest to conjure.

And yet, wizards and witches had to take care. Snapping your fingers, or waving your wand, could sometimes spell danger. Some Conjurations could go wrong. This was especially true when conjuring creatures. If the Conjuration was not carried out to the letter, or the caster was simply being rather silly with their skills, dangerous mistakes such as frog-rabbit creatures could occur.

Can nature itself also conjure something out of "thin air"? And why, in the universe around us, is there something, rather than nothing? Where did it all come from?

The Beginning of Space and Time

Muggle astronomers have found that we live in a changing universe. And it seems that few things are changing faster than our very ideas about the universe. As we talked about in the last chapter, our Muggle ancestors thought the universe stood still in space. The planets might have moved, they thought, but the stars were still. Most of the universe didn't move. Muggle ancestors also thought the universe was quite small, and of course earth-centered. But now, in the twenty-first century, we know we live in a very big universe. It's so big, in fact, that light from the very edge of the universe takes longer than twice the age of the earth to reach our telescopes. That's billions of years. And light can travel 186,000 miles each second, so just imagine how bonkersly big the universe is!

Today, the main Muggle idea about the birth and life of our universe is called the big bang theory. The theory says that the whole universe began in a bubble that was thousands of times smaller than a pinhead. It was hotter and denser than anything we can imagine. Not only that but all times and places were one. The big bang didn't happen in an already existing space. All of space was 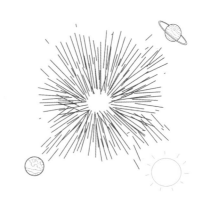 in the big bang. The same goes for place. The big bang didn't happen in a particular place. It happened precisely where you are, and all other places at the same time. And finally, the big bang wasn't an explosion in already existing space. Not in the way we normally think about explosions. Stuff didn't *kaboom* out into space, but stayed where it was, as the surrounding space expanded. It really does sound like the kind of thing that would be conjured up in a Harry Potter story!

How the Universe Might Have Been Simply Conjured

But what happened before the big bang? Was the entire universe simply conjured out of this bubble? Muggle astronomers think so.

They believe that the universe arose out of nothing. Nature, somehow, conjured up the cosmos. (Cosmos is a cool Greek word for universe!)

When the Muggle scholars do the math, they say that our universe started out as a bubble, then expanded into a cosmos. The rest, as they say, is history. But this isn't all they claim. The scholars also think that the universe was conjured out of nothing. We need to talk about what Muggle scholars mean by "nothing." In science, nothing doesn't mean totally empty space, or vacuum. Empty space is in fact rich in energy and tiny particles and antiparticles, which forever appear and disappear within it. So the vacuum of space isn't just an empty space in which things happen. On the other hand, the "nothing" of the big bang was a true nothing. It was a point beyond which space and time did not exist. And yet the cosmos was created!

Finally, why, in this universe of ours, is there something, rather than nothing? Why did the universe, if you believe the big bang theory, simply appear? Muggle astronomers say it happened because the laws of science allowed it. In science, it seems, such an event has a particular probability of just happening. No cause is necessary. And so the cosmos does appear to have been conjured out of nothing!

WHAT IS THE REAL STORY OF THE QUEST FOR THE SORCERER'S STONE?

Yes, it was a legendary Stone with magical powers. They called it the Rufescent Stone, as rufescent means tinged with red. The Stone was indeed rumored to have helped create the Elixir of Life, which made its drinker immortal. And the Stone also helped change any metal into pure gold. The Philosopher's, or Sorcerer's, Stone has a special place in Harry Potter's magical world. The tale told was that the Stone was created by Nicolas Flamel. Flamel was a real-life guy. He lived in Paris, France, in the fourteenth and fifteenth centuries, and sold manuscripts—books written by hand rather than typed.

The Stone Flamel made had a big part in Harry's story. His first battle against Lord Voldemort centered around the Stone, during the 1991–1992 school year. Voldemort had tried to steal the Stone, but was stopped from doing so by Harry, and Voldemort's return to power was delayed. When the Stone was safe and sound, Professor Dumbledore talked to Nicolas

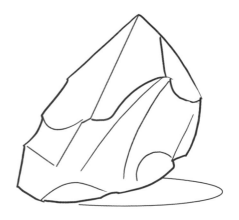

Flamel about the Stone's future. They decided to destroy it. Flamel said he had enough Elixir left to sort his life out, before he and his wife could happily die, after living for over six hundred years!

And yet, there was a twist in the tale of the Stone. Five years after it was destroyed, Harry wondered if a great wizard like Voldemort might find another Stone. Maybe the one created by Flamel was not unique. Or perhaps Voldemort was magically gifted enough to easily make a Stone of his own. Now that we've briefly looked at the Stone in Harry Potter's magical world, what about the real-life Muggle quest to make a Philosopher's Stone?

Making a Philosopher's Stone

The idea of the Philosopher's Stone is part of a branch of Muggle knowledge known as alchemy. Alchemy was an ancient, and often secret, custom with roots all over the world. The people who carried out alchemy—the alchemists—wrote down ways of making a Stone as long ago as the fourth century AD—that's over 1,600 years ago! A number of recipes for making the Stone exist. The recipes depend on the country and culture from which the alchemist came.

Most recipes for making a Stone follow a method known as the Magnum Opus, or the Great Work. To make a Stone, the Opus says the material being worked upon must go through a number of changes in color: *nigredo* (a blackening), *albedo* (a whitening), *citrinitas* (a yellowing), and *rubedo* (a reddening). The Opus also says that bird symbols, such as the raven, the swan, and the phoenix, are used to represent the way the recipe goes through the colors.

Common Metals to Gold

For hundreds of years, the Sorcerer's Stone was the one true prize that alchemists most wanted to make. Around 2,500 years ago, there lived a Greek Muggle thinker named Empedocles (you say his name like this: Em-PED-uh-kleez). Empedocles believed that the whole world is composed of just four elements—earth, air, fire, and water.

After Empedocles, Muggle alchemists began to believe that all material in the world was made of these four elements of earth, air, fire, and water. Some stuff would maybe have more air in it than other material. And other stuff would maybe have more earth and water in it. Muggle alchemists also thought that common metals, such as mercury and lead, could have their amounts of earth, air, fire, and water changed by experiments. And, if your experiments changed the amounts of earth, air, fire, and water so that there was a perfect balance of all four elements, you could transform common metals into gold!

Why Gold?

Why were the alchemists so obsessed with gold? Because they believed gold was better than the other metals due to gold being a perfect balance of earth, air, fire, and water. Today, there are eighty-six known metals. But in ancient times, only seven metals were known: gold, silver, copper, iron, lead, tin, and mercury. We know them now as the Metals of Antiquity, and they would have been familiar to the ancient Muggles of Egypt, Greece, and Rome.

Of these seven metals, gold was the one that captured the Muggle imagination. Gold doesn't tarnish. It keeps its color. And it doesn't crumble. Gold seemed indestructible to ancient Muggles. And yet it could also be easily worked. A single ounce of gold can be beaten to a thin sheet of gold metal almost three hundred feet square! And, of course, its bling is beautiful.

Up until the year 1850, only 10,000 tons of gold had been mined in all of Muggle history. One polar bear weighs around a ton, so the amount of mined gold is the same weight as 10,000 polar bears. That might sound like a lot, but this is all of Muggle history we're talking about! Put another way, a blue whale weighs about 100 tons, so it's the same amount of mined gold as 100 blue whales, in all of Muggle history. You can see why  some Muggles might want to get their hands on more.

In the 1500s and 1600s in Europe, there were many alchemists who came to the royal courts saying they knew the secret to the Philosopher's Stone. So, throughout Europe, alchemists were put to work by princes and kings in the hunt for gold. For the alchemist, it was a good deal—a king or a prince could be persuaded out of huge amounts of money!

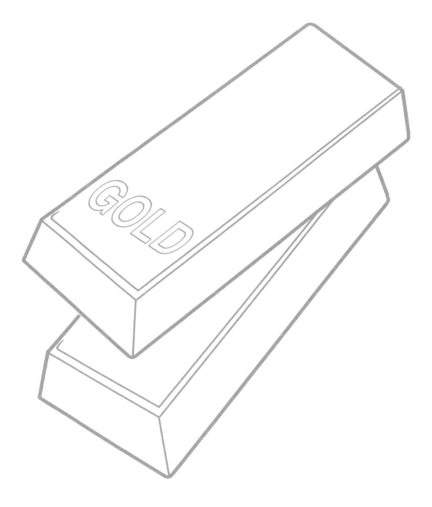

THE DREAM OF ALCHEMY: WHERE DO METALS TRULY TURN INTO GOLD?

"I've never wanted to be a witch, but an alchemist, now that's
a different matter. To invent this wizard world, I've learned
a ridiculous amount about alchemy. Perhaps much of it I'll
never use in the books, but I have to know in detail what
magic can and cannot do."
—J. K. Rowling, being interviewed in the *Herald* (1998)

L et's talk a little bit more about alchemy. In the Harry Potter
world, alchemy is a branch of magic. And, as we have seen, in
the Muggle world it's an ancient science. Ever since that Greek
Muggle Empedocles believed all things were made of the four elements
of earth, air, fire, and water, Muggle alchemists have wanted to make
metals into gold.

So, even in the Muggle world, alchemy has links with "magic." Muggle
alchemy was linked to potion-making and chemistry—the Muggle
"magic" of changing stuff from one form into another. In the wizard

world, as late as the twentieth century, there were still some members of wizard-kind who studied magical alchemy. And Hogwarts was still happy to teach alchemy, assuming there were enough sixth- and seventh-year witches and wizards who wanted to study it.

In the Harry Potter stories, magical alchemy makes itself known to the reader in quiet and gentle ways. For example, ancient Muggle manuscripts about alchemy often talk about the colors of red and white. Some Muggle scholars think that, like common metals and gold, red and white represented two different sides of human nature. And the colors were the reason that J. K. Rowling named Hagrid "Rubeus" (red) and Dumbledore "Albus" (white).

In the Muggle world, the study of alchemy has sat alongside the history of magical alchemy in the Harry Potter stories. The main aims of Muggle alchemy even seem like magic when you read them. Muggle alchemists wanted to make a potion, or elixir, that would make someone live forever. They also wanted to make an alkahest, which is a liquid that would dissolve everything! And, famously, the other aim was chrysopoeia—the making of common metals into precious ones, especially gold. (Chrysopoeia is pronounced like this: Kris-OO-pee-ya.) In the Muggle world, alchemy helped us learn lots about the world in which we live and forged a path for modern science, and especially medicine and chemistry.

Maybe what's not so well-known is the fact that Muggle scientists have realized the dream of chrysopoeia. And that's because, somewhere in our bonkersly big universe, common elements really are being slowly changed into gold.

Making Gold

When the universe was born, only three chemical elements were made: lots of hydrogen and helium, and a dash of lithium. But Muggle scientists think that, ever since then, the stars in the universe have been making all the other elements. That's because stars are the true power of our universe. They are bringers of energy and light. Stars are the building blocks from which the entire cosmos was created. And without our own star there'd be no light, no life, and no earth as we know it. Muggle scientists think that all planets get their light and life from stars like our sun. The sun is a huge ball of burning gas. It's mostly hydrogen gas, but about a quarter of it is made of helium gas. In fact, all stars are made of gas. And their makeup depends on how old they are. Older stars will have a greater amount of gases heavier than hydrogen and helium.

Stars like the sun burn about 4.4 million tons of gas every second. That's as much energy as seven trillion nuclear explosions, every second. As the very center of stars like the sun just sizzles, over ten million degrees of sizzling, it's hot enough to turn hydrogen gas into helium. And that's how "fusion" happens. Most of the stuff in the universe is locked up inside stars. About three-quarters of this stuff is hydrogen, and one-quarter helium. But a tiny 2 percent of the universe is made of what Muggle scientists call the "heavy" elements, like gold.

And so it's the inside of stars where the alchemists' dream comes true. Over billions of years, stars make heavy elements like gold out of the lighter elements, then recycle them back into space by star wind and exploding stars known as supernovae. And that's where Muggle gold comes from. Every gram of gold began billions of years ago, forged out of the inside of an exploding star in a supernova. The gold particles lost into space from the explosion mixed with rocks and dust to form part of the early earth. They've been lying in wait ever since.

WHO WAS THE REAL MERLIN?

"The Order of Merlin, commemorating the most famous wizard of his time, has been given since the fifteenth century. Legend says that the green ribbon, on which the First Class Order hangs, is to reflect Merlin's Hogwarts house."
—J. K. Rowling, *Pottermore* (2019)

Merlin is described in the Harry Potter world as the most famous wizard in all of history. And like many famous people, Merlin's fame had led to his name being part of the everyday language of the wizard world, such as the saying "Merlin's beard!" and the less common "Merlin's pants!"

According to J. K. Rowling, Merlin went to Hogwarts. He was also known as the Prince of the Enchanters and attended the School of Witchcraft and Wizardry during the Middle Ages, which could be any time between the fifth and fifteenth centuries! Not pinning down the date is a good idea. That's because the Merlin legend is one of the most powerful myths

of the English-speaking world. There are rumors his wand was made of old English oak, and that his resting place has never been found, but no one is quite sure when he lived.

Merlin was sorted into Slytherin House. And there are stories that Merlin was taught by Salazar Slytherin himself, one of the four founders of Hogwarts School. Salazar Slytherin's distrust for Muggle-born students led to his leaving the school under a dark cloud. But Merlin believed that wizards and witches should help Muggles and exist peacefully alongside them. This idea fits well with the idea of Merlin in another great book, T. H. White's wonderful *The Once and Future King*, where Merlin the wizard declares, "The Destiny of Man is to unite, not to divide. If you keep on dividing you end up as a collection of monkeys throwing nuts at each other out of separate trees."

In the Harry Potter stories, beliefs like this led to the formation of the Order of Merlin. It started as a group who wanted to stop the use of magic against Muggles. Later, the Order became an award, given to witches and wizards who did great deeds for the good of wizard-kind. But who was the real Merlin?

Magicians of the Middle Ages

Merlin lived in the Middle Ages, but what was he like? Well, at that time, there were men known as philosophers. And Merlin sounds like he would easily fit into their company. One example of such a philosopher was an English scholar named Roger Bacon, who lived around 1235 to 1315 AD. Bacon wanted to understand the ways of the world, through living and thinking. There was also a mysterious philosopher called Peter the Pilgrim. And he sounds a lot like Merlin.

Roger Bacon spent a fortune on doing science experiments. He did so many experiments that the Pope put him in prison for his pains. Meanwhile, Peter the Pilgrim was a pioneer in the study of magnets, and, according to his great admirer Roger Bacon, "He does not care for speeches and battles of words but pursues the works of wisdom and finds peace in them."

Roger Bacon seems to have predicted a future time when the world would see motor ships, motor cars, and airplanes. And yet Bacon was in awe of Peter the Pilgrim. Bacon said this about Peter the Pilgrim:

He knows natural science by experiment, and medicaments and alchemy and all things in the heavens or beneath them, and he would be ashamed if any layman, or old woman or rustic, or soldier should know anything about the soil that he was ignorant of. Whence he is conversant with the casting of metals and the working of gold, silver, and other metals and all minerals; he knows all about soldiering and arms and hunting; he has examined agriculture and land surveying and farming; he has further considered old wives' magic and fortune-telling and the charms of them and of all magicians, and the tricks and illusions of jugglers. But as honour and reward would hinder him from the greatness of his experimental work he scorns them.

This description of Peter the Pilgrim is like one of the earliest stories about Merlin. In 1152 AD, a monk called Geoffrey of Monmouth wrote that Merlin would declare things like this: "I knew the secrets of things and the flight of birds and the wandering motion of the stars and the gliding of the fishes. . . . All this vexed me and denied a natural rest to my human mind."

Merlin the Magician

So who was Merlin? The famous English poet Alfred Tennyson wrote about the great wizard in a poem of 1859. The poem was called "Merlin and Vivien" and it described Merlin like this: "the most famous man of all those times, Merlin, who knew the range of all their arts, Had built the King his havens, ships, and halls, Was also Bard, and knew the starry heavens."

The main place where people got the myths about Merlin was from another book by Geoffrey of Monmouth, written in 1136. The book was a history of ancient Britain. In the book, Geoffrey created a character he named Merlin Ambrosius. It's not that the character of Merlin didn't exist in history. It's just that Geoffrey made Merlin stories out of other stories. Some stories were about Merlinus Caledonensis, a philosopher and wild man with no link to King Arthur. And other stories were about the warrior and leader Ambrosius Aurelianus. Together Geoffrey made them into Merlin Ambrosius.

Geoffrey's tales of the wizard were instantly popular. Later writers then added to the Merlin myths to make more tall tales. In time, the idea of a great wizard was conjured up in the minds of everyone who heard about Merlin. He was a cambion, which means a kind of Mudblood, born of a woman, but whose father was an incubus, a nonhuman from whom Merlin got his supernatural powers and skills. In later accounts, Merlin helps with the birth of the legendary King Arthur through the use of magic. Later still, stories told of Merlin as an adviser to Arthur, and of

Merlin being bewitched and locked up by the Lady of the Lake. And that Merlin even created Stonehenge!

So what do the tales of Merlin mean in history? Merlin's legend comes from a dark time for science. People had become narrow-minded and superstitious. But Merlin was close to nature and understood the ways of the world. Water and islands were thought to be magical. And wise old sages like Merlin knew of that old magic, the old ways of nature, and the kaleidoscope of a future that science would one day bring.

WHO REALLY WAS THE LAST GREAT WIZARD?

"The name of [Gellert] Grindelwald is justly famous: in a list of Most Dangerous Dark Wizards of All Time, he would miss out on the top spot only because You-Know-Who arrived, a generation later, to steal his crown. . . . Educated at Durmstrang, a school famous even then for its unfortunate tolerance of the Dark Arts, Grindelwald showed himself quite as precociously brilliant as Dumbledore."
—Rita Skeeter, *The Life and Lies of Albus Dumbledore* (1997)

Who was the last great wizard? Professor Albus Dumbledore, perhaps? Dumbledore was famous for the discovery of the twelve uses of dragon's blood and his work on alchemy. Or maybe, if you like your wizards on the dark and Death Eater side, you favor Tom Marvolo Riddle, later known as Lord Voldemort? Riddle was the most powerful of Dark Wizards. He said he pushed the boundaries of magical forces further than ever before.

But, in the Muggle world, the last great, and often dark, wizard was Isaac Newton. What did Newton conjure up? Many Muggles believe Newton almost single-handedly conjured up modern science. He uncovered the laws that govern the cosmos. He made up new branches of math, understood the makeup of light, and worked out the laws of gravity and motion that control the entire universe.

But Newton had a weird side. He died in 1727. And over two hundred years later in 1936, a huge collection of Newton's private papers was put up for sale in London. The papers had been kept from the public for those two centuries. Many of the papers were bought by a man called John Maynard Keynes, who was an expert on money. Keynes found that many of Newton's papers were written in a secret code. And for six years, Keynes tried to decode them.

Keynes hoped they would show the private thoughts of Newton—the father of modern science. But what the code showed was another, far darker, side to Newton's work. In the manuscripts Keynes found a Newton unknown to the rest of the world, a man obsessed with the books of the Christian Bible and who practiced the occult, which is the study of magical powers, such as witchcraft.

The Alchemist

It's important to know something about Newton's story. Like Harry Potter himself, Newton lived in troublesome times. In Newton's time, England saw the Great Fire of London and the black death. And if that wasn't bad enough, a civil war had meant the death of 190,000 of his countryfolk, out of a total population of only five million. It's true that Newton helped bring a new age of science. But that wasn't the whole story about Newton.

The secret papers showed a very different man. For example, in the year Newton became a professor at Cambridge, he also bought two furnaces, a hodgepodge of chemicals, and a curious collection of books. Newton had found alchemy.

Alchemy at the time had been outlawed. In these troublesome times of confusion and crisis, the English government feared that alchemists would ruin the country's money system with fake gold. So, if you got caught doing alchemy, you were swiftly and severely punished. Some alchemists were punished by being hanged on a gilded scaffold. And sometimes alchemists were made to wear suits of tinsel as they were hanged to make it even more of a public spectacle.

The Great Fire of London and the black death were making life in London pretty tough. So Newton moved to Cambridge and threw himself into his alchemy. But he wasn't looking to make himself rich. He simply wanted to know the mind of God, as Newton believed alchemy was a direct route to God himself. Alchemy tried to answer questions such as "What is the Earth?" "What is the cosmos made of?" "What is matter made of?" And Newton really wanted to know.

He read the most ancient texts in search of his answers. Newton believed that the Ancient Greeks knew great truths about nature and the cosmos but that this Muggle wisdom had been lost over time. Newton actually believed he was God's messenger on planet Earth. He thought it was his job to find the secret codes hidden in both the Bible and the Greek myths, which he thought were alchemy recipes disguised in code.

Gravity

Alchemy was not Newton's only obsession. One day Newton's friend Edmond Halley, a Muggle astronomer, asked Newton what kind of curve the planets would follow in their orbits around the sun. At the time, Muggle astronomers had started to think that the planets were attracted to the sun by some strange kind of force. Halley's question to Newton was to change the world forever.

For the next eighteen months, Newton worked on the question of how the planets move through space. He barely ate or slept, and saw next to no one. Finally came Newton's five-hundred-page masterpiece, the *Principia Mathematica*. It was the greatest book of Muggle science ever written. Not only was the *Principia* the most magnificent work, but it was also the most daring Muggle science book ever written.

Newton's book was about a theory of everything in the universe. He saw that many moving things had a common cause. Maybe it was the moon's orbit around the earth, or the motion of the moons around Jupiter, or a cannonball's motion on earth. But Newton saw that they were all ruled by the same law of gravity. In a revolutionary leap, Newton said that this mysterious and invisible force was everywhere in the cosmos. And the law became known as Newton's law of gravitation.

So Muggles say the last great wizard was not Dumbledore, or Voldemort. It was Isaac Newton. He had brilliantly conjured the tricks of the trade from every Muggle field in which he worked. He was an ingenious and energetic builder who dabbled in the dark stuff, as well as the light. He was astonishingly brilliant in great books like the *Principia*, and in the genius of his daring experiments. He was so clever, in fact, that a Muggle writer called Richard Westfall, who wrote one of the most famous books about Newton's life, said this: "The end result of my study of Newton has served to convince me that with him there is no measure. He has become for me wholly other, one of the tiny handful of supreme geniuses who have shaped the categories of human intellect."

HOW WOULD HERMIONE'S TIME-TURNER WORK?

I mark the hours, every one, Nor have I yet outrun the Sun. My use and value, unto you, Are gauged by what you have to do.
—Inscription on Hermione Granger's borrowed Time-Turner

Picture this: Hermione is standing at the Crucifixion. Spellbound, and openmouthed, she can't help but stare at the scene. Perhaps the most famous in all of history. This, she thought, is one of the benefits of time travel. Being able to feel, firsthand, history in the making. Just a few things she must remember: Mainly, don't do anything to disrupt history. (Hermione says to herself: *no stone throwing this time!*) She then remembers something else: when the crowd is asked who should be saved, she should join in with the call, "Give us Barabbas!"

Suddenly, Hermione realizes what's weird and witchy about the crowd. Not a single soul from 33 AD is actually present. The mob condemning poor Jesus to the cross is made up (lock, stock, and smoking wand) of witches and wizards from the future.

But the scene is not just littered with wizard-kind. By being here as time travelers, they've actually changed the outcome of history itself. The wizards and witches think they know the way the story is meant to go.

Rather than Jesus being set free, the crowd is meant to choose Barabbas, the bandit. But history only goes that way because wizard-kind are witness to the scene! Would Jesus have been set free instead, if they hadn't interfered?

This story is just the kind of chaos the Ministry of Magic wanted to avoid when witches and wizards used the Time-Turner, the most common wizard means of time travel.

Time-Turners

According to the Harry Potter stories, the Time-Turner looked like an hourglass on a necklace. And how far you traveled back in time depended on how many times the hourglass was turned. Typical Time-Turners, supplied by the Ministry of Magic, had an Hour-Reversal Charm worked into them. This Hour-Reversal Charm, trapped in with the device, meant that the longest time travel journey was around five hours. Any longer than that, and the traveler might come to some harm.

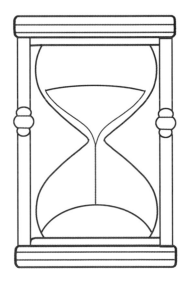

There was also a time device known as a "true" Time-Turner. These devices meant the traveler could visit whatever time they liked, and way beyond the five-hour time limit. But few travelers ever survived such journeys. Trials with "true" Time-Turners ended in 1899, when traveler Eloise Mintumble got trapped, for five days, in 1402 AD. Her body aged five centuries when it returned to the present and was fatally wounded.

Professor McGonagall gave Hermione a Time-Turner so she could attend more studies than the Hogwarts timetable would allow. At the end of the school year, Hermione and Harry also used it to travel in time to save Sirius Black and Buckbeak from certain death.

The idea of time travel is popular in many types of stories, not just Harry Potter tales in which a Time-Turner is used for travel. Muggle scientist Professor Stephen Hawking refused to believe time travel is possible. His argument went something like this: "If time travel really IS possible, then where are the time tourists of the future? Why aren't they visiting us, telling us all about the joys of time travel?"

Time-Turner Tunnels

How would a Time-Turner work? One way is through the creation of a wormhole. A wormhole is like a kind of bridge or tunnel through space. If you make a wormhole, then the region of space where the wormhole sits is warped, or bent. It's basically a shortcut in space and time through which you can travel. Trouble is, time travelers would not be able to travel back in time to a date before the wormhole was made. So, imagine a witch or wizard made a wormhole on April 1, 1666. That would mean they couldn't go back in time before April 1, 1666.

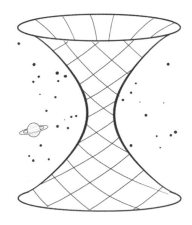

What do these wormholes look like? They're the kind of swirly cosmic tunnel you often see in movies during a journey through space and time. Real wormholes may have at least two mouths, connected to a single tunnel. And Muggle scientists really do believe they exist. At least in theory. And, as that theory belongs to Albert Einstein, Muggles take it pretty seriously. People and things may travel from one mouth to the other by passing through the wormhole. Muggles haven't found one yet, but the universe is huge. And we haven't really been looking very long!

WHAT KIND OF PROPHECY
IS POSSIBLE?

In the Harry Potter world, a prophecy was a prediction made by a Seer. The Seer, a gifted wizard or witch who was able to see into the future, would suddenly start saying the prophecy without really knowing it. Then, they would go into a type of trance, speaking strangely in a changed voice.

A record of prophecy was then kept in a spun-glass orb and known as a Prophecy Record. The Prophecy Records, round orbs that seemed to contain clouds of swirling mist, were stored in the Hall of Prophecies, and kept within the Department of Mysteries. Only members of wizard-kind mentioned in the Prophecy were allowed to remove that record from the Hall. Many Prophecy Records were destroyed in the Battle of the Department of Mysteries.

One of the most famous Seers was Professor Sybill Trelawney. She was the Head of Divination at Hogwarts School. Professor Trelawney's first recorded prophecy was witnessed by Albus Dumbledore. The prophecy foretold the birth of a wizard who would be capable of defeating Lord Voldemort. The prophecy went on to say that Voldemort would mark this young wizard "as his equal," and that either the young wizard, or Voldemort, would eventually kill the other. This boy, of course, was shown to be Harry Potter. Harry knew nothing of the Prophecy until Dumbledore told him the tale, after the Battle of the Department of Mysteries. The prophecy proved to be true.

But is prophecy in the Muggle world possible? And, if not, what's the closest we Muggles can come to prophecy?

Muggle Prophecy

If we are to find prophecy anywhere in the Muggle world, it will probably be in science. Science is different from most other studies because science is about how things are done. And if you know how things are done, you may be able to tell what will happen in the future. It will help if you think about science as a recipe for doing things. Science is a kind of recipe that tells you how to carry out certain tasks, should you need to do them, and what will happen when you do so. Like wanting to fly in the sky like a bird or on a broomstick, for example. Science made its own recipe for that, and Muggles finally found out how to fly.

Earlier in the book we talked about the last great wizard being Muggle scientist Isaac Newton. He was the Muggle who came up with a "theory of everything" with his theory of gravity. Newton's theory thought of the universe as if it were clockwork. He thought that all things in existence could be explained in terms of motion and that they would be easily open to prediction and even prophecy.

But Muggles after Newton found that there was a lot of chaos is nature. Things you couldn't really predict, like sudden tsunamis rising up out of the sea, for example, or that huge space rock that bashed into planet Earth and killed off the poor dinosaurs. So Newton's laws were okay if you wanted to predict where the planets would be in their orbit, and send spaceships sailing to Saturn. That kind of thing. But there are many things about the world that science isn't so good at predicting. The air racing around an airplane's wing is one such example. Or blood, coursing through the heart. Or climate change. The behavior of complicated systems like weather and climate is hard to predict. Even if Muggles could understand it, they still wouldn't be able to make precise predictions. Weather is almost impossible to predict, as you may  know if you've ever been caught by surprise by a random rain shower. And that's because the weather's behavior depends very much on starting conditions, and those tiny differences become hugely boosted by the weather system.

So chaos makes it hard for Muggles to make prophecy. Because of the millions of tiny imperfections in systems like the weather, tiny differences soon become huge changes in the way things turn out. Soon enough, the imperfections overpower our careful Muggle calculations. And even simple systems can be hard to predict. So, in fact, it turns out Muggles can't really predict more than a few seconds into the future!

PART II
TECHNICAL TRICKERY AND PARAPHERNALIA

COULD SCIENTISTS BE THE MODERN WIZARDS AND WITCHES?

"We do not need magic to change the world, we carry
all the power we need inside ourselves already: we have
the power to imagine better."
—J. K. Rowling, *Very Good Lives: The Fringe Benefits of Failure
and the Importance of Imagination* (2008)

Are there wizards and witches living in the world today? And, if there are, what kind of Muggles might be able to levitate things, without using the Wingardium Leviosa spell? What type of Muggle might make something fly, without the use of a broomstick? And what Muggles might make something scary into something quite silly, without the need for the Riddikulus spell? The short answer, dear reader, is scientists. Muggle scientists are the modern wizards and witches. And here's why.

First up, think about magic and science. How are they similar? We've already seen that science, like magic, is a recipe for doing things, right? And, like magic, science is really, really old. It started thousands of years ago, and has changed a lot since, of course. But you may be surprised to learn that magic and science share a common beginning.

Science has been the most powerful thing to totally change our world. In ancient times, science was done by Muggles who wanted to shape the world in which they lived. Imagine living thousands, or even a million, years ago. Life was hard. And nature was red in tooth and claw, as a famous Muggle poet once said. Life was dangerous! Your entire life was spent just struggling to stay alive. If it's not the dangerous predators stalking you at night, it's the constant search for food in the day. Where will your next meal come from?

Knowing How Nature Works

All those thousands of years ago, Muggles had little to help them survive except their imaginations. When thinking about their next meal, Muggles had a huge choice of plants and animals to pick from. But which were okay to eat? And which were poisonous? It was hard to tell. Not only that, but if Muggles then went on a journey to help themselves survive, as they often did, then the plants and animals might be different in the new place where they lived. Muggles relied on nature and needed to understand it. So Muggles with an imagination thought about the ways in which they could try to understand nature. It was important, as any mistakes could end in death!

Think about fire, for example. Fire was a very useful tool for ancient Muggles. Fire helped keep away any looming killer creatures, especially at night. At night, sitting around a campfire was the safest place to be. Fire could also smoke out those annoying biting insects. And fire could help cook more food to eat. Muggles with imagination would see the flames made by lightning, say, or from forest fires, or even a volcano. And somehow, they were able to catch and control the flames. When Muggles first caught fire like this (not that they were actually *on* fire!) they learned a lot. They learned how to cook, which taught them some chemistry. And learning to cook plants and animals also taught them some biology.

Muggles Used "Magic," Too

But tools like fire could help the Muggles only so much. So, to try and control nature even more, some Muggles again used their imaginations. They pretended to be the animals they were trying to hunt. In other words, Muggles used animals as "magic totems." A Muggle tribe would use images of the totem, or maybe symbols and even dances, to try and make the animal healthy and easy for them to catch and eat. The Muggle that "became" the animal totem is called the Animagus. And, in a way, an Animagus is like an early magician. The Muggle tribe believed that, as long as the rules of the magic totem were followed, the tribe would stay alive and do well.

The Muggle tribes soon thought that the totems had special powers. The totems became important to the Muggles. The totems had to be treated well, or else the balance of nature would be upset. And so the totem had a special power over Muggles. Totem symbols still exist. Just think of the lion of Gryffindor, the serpent of Slytherin, the badger of Hufflepuff, and the eagle of Ravenclaw.

Theory of Magic Spirits

So Muggles tried to copy or mimic the workings of the world. We know this as we have found evidence in the caves of Europe. One example is the cave paintings of the Trois-Frères in the Ariège department of southwestern France. The art on the walls of these caves shows that there were already magicians fifteen thousand years ago, when Muggles think this cave art was first painted. A painting

there, known as "the sorcerer," shows a Muggle wearing the horns of a stag, an owl mask, wolf ears, the forelegs of a bear, and the tail of a horse! And Muggles think the sorcerer was painted as his Animagus behavior was trying to make sure the tribe had a successful hunt. It was important to the tribe to make art about the Animagus.

What was the Animagus doing? They were using a likeness of the animal the tribe was trying to hunt. The Muggles thought it would make the hunt a success. Later they used symbols, thinking that if they did something with the symbol, for example, make the animal symbol offer up itself to the Muggles, then this would also happen in real life when they hunted the animal. Later still, the magic of symbols became a magic of spirits. The idea was that a spirit was a thing in nature, like the wind or the sun, and that if you conjured the spirits, you might also be able to control the wind and sun to your advantage. Much later in history, the idea of the spirit became very important in how Muggles thought about things in science, such as gases like oxygen, which Muggles breathe to stay alive!

So science and magic shared a common beginning. At the start, the "magic" would have been done by most of the tribe. But later, as that cave art in France shows, the animal magic was done by a single Muggle, known as the Animagus, who seems to have some special place in the tribe. In such tribes today, there are still special Muggles like this, members of the tribe who do the "magic" medicine. They are very respected by the tribe, as the other Muggles believe the "magician" has a special relationship with nature and the world around us. They are a little bit separate from the normal work of the tribe. And the Muggles believe their magical arts are good for the tribe. Magicians were keepers of learning and knowledge. And they were the ancestors of the modern-day Muggle philosophers and scientists.

COULD SCIENCE MAKE MOODY'S MAD EYE?

Who gets your vote for the most badass wizard? Okay, let's not count Dumbledore, Voldemort, or Snape in the vote. They're probably in most Muggles' top three wizards. Who do we have left as the main contenders? Maybe you'd cast your vote for Sirius Black, the Animagus? Or perhaps Gellert Grindelwald, the brilliantly talented (and brilliantly named!) wielder of the Elder Wand known as the Second Most Powerful Dark Wizard of All Time. That's some title to conjure with.

Or perhaps your pick of the wizardy crop is Alastor "Mad-Eye" Moody. Mad-Eye Moody was a master of magic. Many thought he was the most powerful Auror of all time. In the First Wizarding War and its aftermath, Mad-Eye battled and defeated dozens of deadly Death Eaters. And Voldemort thought Mad-Eye was such a deadly enemy that he made Moody his main target, of all the talented wizards and witches protecting Harry during the Battle of the Seven Potters.

As his name suggests, Moody was most famous for his magical Eye. The magical Eye had been put in instead of an eye that Moody had lost in battle. The new Eye was electric blue and sat in Moody's otherwise empty eye socket. The Eye could swivel through all directions in Moody's head. It enabled him to spy through anything, whether it was wood, cloaks of invisibility, or even through the back of his own mad head! In fact, the Eye seems to have been made just for Moody, as when Barty Crouch Jr. wore it, the Eye got stuck in mid-whirl.

What was the Eye's full range of function? In the movie version of *Harry Potter and the Goblet of Fire*, the Eye was seen to have a zoom function. And the fact that the Eye was powerful enough to see through the Cloak of Invisibility, one of the Deathly Hallows, suggests that it may have been a very rare artifact indeed. The Cloak, according to legend, granted the owner true invisibility. As the origin of the Eye was never known, perhaps the Eye was itself an ancient and very powerful artifact, matching the Deathly Hallows if not in fame then certainly in power.

The Muggle Mad-Eye

So what are the chances of Muggles making something like a Mad-Eye? Well, Muggles have already made artificial eyes that can be used to help blind people see. The artificial eyes work like this. Outside the person's eye, usually on a pair of glasses, the person wears a camera. This camera feeds an image back into the eye and helps the eye understand light, shape, and movement. The picture they get isn't quite as good as normal eyesight. The Muggle with the artificial eye can see the edges of things, and in black and white only. That's because the working of the real eye socket is damaged, which means the poor Muggle has lost the ability to see light and color. But by using the artificial eye, the Muggle brain can learn how to make sense of the signals, and convert them into images. The Muggle users of the artificial eye are then able to read books, cross the street, or see images of their Muggle family for the first time in years.

Muggle engineers all over the world are now working to make "Muggle Mad-Eyes" even better than before. The next generation of eyes will be able to see color. They will use a special computer program that will change camera data into sharper images, and be able to change things like focus and brightness. If things go according to plan, in the next five years there could  be new Muggle eyes that are as good as, or even better than, natural eyes.

Looking even further into the future, Muggles have cool plans for artificial eyes! They want to make an eye that will be able to bypass the eye socket and feed data straight into the brain. This revolution in eye technology could mean a huge improvement for millions of Muggles whose eyesight needs help. Sure, this new Muggle eye may not be able to see through wood, cloaks of invisibility, or the back of a Muggle head, but the device may give some Muggles almost superhuman eyesight!

This is what the future Muggle eye might be able to do. For one thing, it could have sight like a telescope, which means it will be able to zoom in, just like Moody's Mad-Eye in the movies. Muggle brains might be able to learn how to read this telescope data, so they can have the same powerful zoom functions as cameras. And that means Muggle eye wearers could learn to see much closer, or farther, than the normal Muggle eye.

What's more, the future Muggle eye might be able to see more of the spectrum than just the usual visible light. The Muggle eye might see not only the colors such as red, through orange, yellow, green, blue, and indigo, to violet, but also infrared. Infrared is the kind of light that television remotes use. So a Muggle eye might be able to sense heat, detect some gases, and even have the ability to see through objects! In microscope mode, the Muggle eye might be able to see the millions of creeping microbes living on the Muggle body. And, as the eye will never sleep, it could be set to guard us at all times of day, and wake you at night if danger looms, or if light dawns outside. As the Muggle eye would also have Wi-Fi, the Muggle wearer could record their day-to-day life and beam it straight online. (Uh oh. Not such a good idea.) But check this: your favorite movie or program could be streamed straight to your brain, totally skipping TV!

Today, the Muggle eye sees only a tiny part of the spectrum. We see only one part in a hundred, or around 1 percent of the spectrum. That's not a lot of this big old world, when you think about it. But, in a future where Muggles become cyborgs and have artificial eyes, their experience of the world might be even better than Mad-Eye Moody's!

WHEN WILL MUGGLES MAKE MOVING PORTRAITS?

"Hogwarts portraits are able to talk and move around from picture to picture. They behave like their subjects. However, the degree to which they can interact with the people looking at them depends not on the skill of the painter, but on the power of the witch or wizard painted."
—J. K. Rowling, *Pottermore* (2019)

In the magic world, family photos were very different from Muggle ones. Magical portraits could walk and talk. The witches and wizards in the photo might even move from frame to frame! Good Muggle photography depends on the look and feel of the person being photographed, as the person in the frame didn't move. But, in the Harry Potter world, magical portraits actually moved and behaved like their subjects. And the amount a magical portrait impressed the viewer was not so much to do with how good the photographer was, but more to do with the power of the magical sitter being photographed.

Good Muggle photography is meant to capture what the person in the picture is like in real life. But the magical art of photography went one step further. When a magical portrait was taken, some of the sitter's character (what they were like, maybe their favorite phrases, and the way they walked) was captured to make sure the art was a true likeness. For example, the portrait of Sir Cadogan was always challenging the viewer to a fight, or was forever falling off its horse. Or the Fat Lady portrait at the Gryffindor tower entrance, which forever adored good food, drink and the highest security, long after the Fat Lady herself had passed away into witchy history.

In the Harry Potter stories, the idea of magical portraits was brilliantly changed to suit the plot. Take *Harry Potter and the Goblet of Fire*, for example. The story begins with gossip in a local tavern where the people in the portraits move from frame to frame, playing the telephone game with the latest rumors. At more festive times, when the wine flowed and the living was easy, the subjects of the portraits got a little drunk! In another tale, when Hogwarts had a spring clean, the portraits complained about the cleaning and grumped about their skin feeling a little raw. And in *Harry Potter and the Prisoner of Azkaban*, the Fat Lady became an important part of the plot when knife slashes were found in her frame.

There were magical rules for most moving portraits. They were not able to do whatever they liked. Magical portraits didn't really reveal too much about the details of the lives of the witches and wizards in the frame. Like Muggle photos, the magical portraits were more like a moving snapshot of a wizard or witch, as seen by the artist.

But there were some rare and special magical portraits that were able to do more. These special few portraits had more interaction with events in the living world. Just think about the portraits at Hogwarts of headmasters or headmistresses painted before their deaths. Once the portrait was done, the head teacher was able to store his or her portrait away. But they could also visit it and tell the interactive portrait how to act and behave just like himself or herself. And so the head teachers taught their own portraits! They gave the paintings much knowledge and many useful memories that could be handy to other future head teachers! And this meant, with all the portraits kept in the office, the head teacher had lots of wisdom to help run Hogwarts. It would be wrong to think of the head teacher's office as a sleepy place, as lots was going on in those magical portraits!

The Muggle Moving Portrait

What progress has been made in making moving portraits in the Muggle world? There is, of course, the GIF. GIFs have wobbled across thousands of webpages, fluttered within thousands of Facebook profiles, and transformed lots of Tumblrs. GIFs can be seen in advertising, the sign-off signatures of email, and social media avatars. GIFs are everywhere!

"GIF" stands for "graphics interchange format." The GIF was developed by Steve Wilhite of CompuServe in June 1987. The GIF began as black-and-white image transfers. Then they moved to 256 colors, but still take up small amounts of computer space so they're easy to use. GIFs are very popular. Lots of Muggles use them as a way of making funny remarks on social media, or maybe for promoting the latest viral YouTube videos.

Will the GIF ever make it into Muggle newspapers? Will they start to look like the magical portraits in wizarding world newspapers such as the *Daily Prophet* and the *New York Ghost*? *Empire* magazine has been inspired by the Harry Potter world. It made the Muggle world's first-ever moving-image cover. The edition of the magazine was about the launch of the Harry Potter spin-off movie *Fantastic Beasts and Where to Find Them*.

The magazine cover looked something like an enchanted newspaper, and was modeled on the *New York Ghost* newspaper from the *Fantastic Beasts* story. The *Empire* images move, with two portraits embedded into the magazine cover.

How does it work? There is technology hidden in the magazine cover. There's a twin layer of thick paper, or card, and inside that an embedded video screen. This lets the magazine reader press play on the portraits. The cover hides all the microchips and circuit boards needed to make the portraits come to life, simply by pressing a button. It may not yet be a true Muggle version of a magical portrait, but it's a start!

HOW COULD YOU MAKE YOUR OWN MARAUDER'S MAP TO SKIP CLASS?

Picture yourself on a wet Wednesday afternoon. You're trapped in business studies, the most tedious topic known to any school syllabus. No need to panic. A cunning plan is afoot. And it involves a magic map. Outside your tutorial of torture lies a network of classrooms and corridors. Your mission, should you choose to accept it, is to somehow find your way through the chaos of corridors and escape into the life-giving sunshine, way beyond the school security cameras.

But wait, what exactly does this magic map do? In the Harry Potter world, the Marauder's Map was one such magical document. With this map, a way through the maze of complicated corridors of Hogwarts could be found. After all, Hogwarts was a seven-storied, one hundred and forty-two staircased, towered, turreted, and deep-dungeoned beast of a building.

The map was an "all-seeing eye" into the medieval castle's deep, dark heart. The map spied each and every classroom, all hallways, and every castle corner. The castle grounds also fell under the map's gaze, as well as all those creepy corridors, hidden within its walls. The map's magic sight also spied on witches and wizards within the castle. Each one was shown on the map by a moving set of footprints and a scroll-like caption. The Marauder's Map wasn't even fooled by Harry's invisibility cloak, Animagi, or Polyjuice Potions. It even spied the many ghosts of the school.

But the map wasn't perfect. It couldn't distinguish between wizards or witches with the same name, for example. And it didn't show some rooms. The Room of Requirement was found by Dobby the house elf, and not the map itself, which seemed not to even know the Room existed! The same was true of the Chamber of Secrets. It never appeared on the map. The Chamber may not have shown simply because the map's creators, Remus Lupin, Peter Pettigrew, Sirius Black, and James Potter—also known as Messrs Moony, Wormtail, Padfoot, and Prongs, "Purveyors of Aids to Magical Mischief-Makers"—simply never knew of its existence.

The magical Marauder's Map sounds like a lot of fun. So what would we need to make a Muggle version?

Tagging Teacher

A Muggle version of the Marauder's Map might be based on something called GPS. GPS stands for Global Positioning System. GPS is a network of around thirty satellites that orbit our planet at a height of about 12,500 miles. The GPS system was first developed by the US military. But in time, any Muggle with a GPS device was allowed to use it. So, whether a Muggle has SatNav, a cell phone, or a plain GPS unit, they can receive the radio signals that are sent out by the thirty satellites.

No matter where you are on earth, GPS will find you. Wherever you may roam, at least four GPS satellites are "visible." Each of the satellites sends you data about where it is, and when it is. These data signals, beaming down at the speed of light, are picked up by your GPS, which does the math about just how far away each satellite is, based on the time it took for the beamed message to arrive.

Once the data is done for at least three satellites, your GPS knows where you are. Your GPS device does this using something called, wait for it, trilateration! What's trilateration? Well, imagine using GPS in your school escape situation. And imagine a teacher is lurking somewhere within the school corridors. High in the sky above sit the beady eyes of three satellites. Let's call them satellites A, B, and C. If the lurking teacher is spied by satellite A, then that satellite will know just how far away he is. And if satellites B and C also spy the teacher, they too will read his position. So, taking all three readings together, where they cross is the exact spot of the lurking teacher. And the more satellites there are above the horizon, the more exact will be the reading of the teacher's position.

The good news is that the tech for tagging teacher is already with us. GPS security tags, used for tracking pets, people, or even troublesome teachers, are already on the market. They are tiny, and solar-powered. They are accurate to the meter, and also work indoors. They use a super sensitive antenna, and are smaller than two flat batteries. And these GPS security tags use the satellite constellation.

All this means that your school escape is on. Armed with a smartphone, a school escapee can easily plot current and previous positions of teachers simply by using a mapping app. But one last challenge remains. How do you actually get the GPS tags on the teachers?!

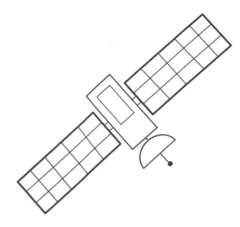

HOW COULD YOU MAKE
A WEASLEY FAMILY CLOCK?

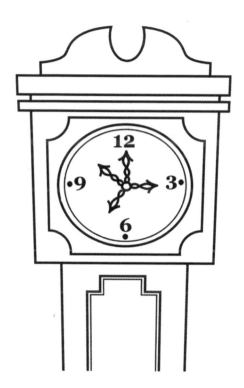

People have a habit of simply vanishing. Famous Chinese thinker Laozi mysteriously disappeared. He vanished in 531 BC, leaving behind his famous philosophy book the *Tao Te Ching*. Spartacus, leader of the slave rebellion against the Roman Republic, also disappeared in a puff of smoke in 71 BC. And Amelia Earhart, the famous American aviator, disappeared on July 2, 1937, after becoming the first woman to attempt a flight around the world.

But vanishing like this was never a problem for the Weasley family in the Harry Potter stories. And that's because they had the famous Weasley Clock. This was no normal time device. It didn't tell the time. Instead, the Weasley Clock told tales about where each Weasley family member was. It was kept in the living room of The Burrow, the Weasley family home on the outskirts of Ottery St Catchpole in Devon, England.

The Clock had nine golden hands, one hand for each member of the household. It was the hands that told the tale of where each Weasley was. And set out on the Clock's face were a set of locations, including School, Work, Travelling, Home, Lost, Hospital, Prison, and even Mortal Peril. There were also fun locations like "time to make tea" (this is England, of course), "time to feed the chickens," and "you're late." Each family member's whereabouts could be seen at a glance, as their assigned Clock hand would be pointing to wherever on earth they were.

Given his liking for all things Muggle, was the head of the household, Arthur Weasley, ever tempted to make something similar for the non-magic market? And, if he did, what tech might he use to do the job?

Wizard Clocks

Believe it or not, "wizardy" Muggle clocks have already been built. So let's go through such a build. First up, an overview. As with the Weasley Clock, our Wizard Clock will have clock hands for people, and clock "times" for places they might be. So our Wizard Clock will also give an at-a-glance guide to the whereabouts of family or friends. And the kind of magic our Clock will use will be a Muggle tech that runs from smartphone to Web-server computer to Wizard Clock. You'll have enough of an idea of where your loved ones are, so you will either be able to stalk them for fun, or know when it's best not to call.

Surely, the dream Wizard Clock of choice is a grandfather clock, set in a wooden frame. Since the Clock has to show people and places, we need to start with a normal two-handed clock then add as many hands as we need. But, for now, let's say we'll make a grand total of four hands, one hand for each of the four houses of Hogwarts: a Professor Dumbledore hand to represent Gryffindor, a luminous Luna Lovegood hand for Ravenclaw, a Professor Pomona Sprout hand for Hufflepuff, and finally a Professor Snape hand for Slytherin.

Our Wizard Clock-face should also show the most commonly used locations. Let's pick some cool places for each of our four hands. As Dumbledore has a keen interest in the heavens, with his own telescope in the Headmaster's Office, let's have a first location of "Astronomy Tower." The wonderfully dotty witch Luna Lovegood lives in a rook-like house in Ottery St Catchpole, so let's name our second location "Ottery." Pomona Sprout is often found pottering around in the Hogwarts Herbology greenhouses, so our third Clock location will be "Greenhouses." And finally, Severus Snape is a very talented Potions Master, so our last Clock location shall be "Dungeons," where he conjures up potions and elixirs. In short, we have four weirdly named Clock locations of Astronomy Tower, Ottery, Greenhouses, and Dungeons! To these we will also add the normal locations of Traveling, Lost, and possibly even Mortal Peril.

A Weasley Clock managed its own magic, of course. But our Wizard Clock needs the help of Muggle tech. Dumbledore, Lovegood, Sprout, and Snape, who together sound like a set of solicitors from a Roald Dahl story, would each need to carry some kind of cell phone. That means they would also have an Android or iOS app, which would know where in the world the cell phone owner was. The apps would mean that, wherever the user roamed, a signal of where they are in the world is sent.

Their whereabouts would wing their way to a Web server—a computer, or program, that beams out data. In our case, the data would be sent to our Wizard Clock. Once the data is collected by the Clock's Wi-Fi, the Clock has four motors that enable it to whiz about and show where each witch and wizard are. And so, like the Weasley Clock, our Wizard Clock has done the deal: the whereabouts of Dumbledore, Lovegood, Sprout, and Snape can be seen at a glance, as our Clock hands will show exactly where they are.

Finally, maybe the real test of our Wizard Clock is the question of Mortal Peril. How are we going to cope with that, using only Muggle tech? Perhaps the best way is to get our wizards and witches to wear some tech on their bodies. A smartwatch, for example, can carry an app that is able to detect whether the wearer of the watch is in stress or danger. The app could pick up signs of whether the witch or wizard wearer was going through changed levels of 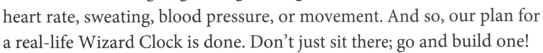 heart rate, sweating, blood pressure, or movement. And so, our plan for a real-life Wizard Clock is done. Don't just sit there; go and build one!

PART III
HERBOLOGY, ZOOLOGY, AND POTIONS

IS THE BEZOAR
A REAL ANTIDOTE?

There are plenty of drinks that can make a Muggle senseless. The spirit drink absinthe has been known to give Muggles hallucinations. Bruichladdich is a very pure and very strong whiskey. And Spirytus Rektyfikowany (imagine getting that in a spelling test!) is a Polish vodka that makes you meet your god when you drink too much!

But the drink that almost did in Ron Weasley was a plain old oak-matured mead, a drink made by fermenting honey. Ron's mead was poisoned. Ron's glass hit the floor first. Ron followed. He crumpled to his knees, tumbled onto a rug, spasmed spookily, and as foam oozed out of his mouth, his skin turned blue.

Harry to the rescue. Looking about, and leaping up, Harry hurriedly stripped the walls of its potions. A box fell forward. Out spilled a scattering of stones, each no bigger than a bird's egg. Harry took one of the dry and shriveled stones, opened Ron's jaw, and thrust it into his throat. At once, Ron stopped moving. But soon, a great hiccupping cough, and Ron is back, living and breathing.

The quick-thinking Harry had used a bezoar. The bezoar was an undigested clump of matter, taken from the gut of a goat. Clumps like this can collect in animal guts. They're usually made of hair and plant material, and are similar to a cat hairball. In the magic world, bezoars were used as antidotes to most poisons, though they didn't work on basilisk venom. But bezoars are also real-life Muggle objects. So, what's fact, and what's fiction? What exactly are they, and what can they actually do?

Bezoars

Bezoars were believed for many centuries to be the most marvelous Muggle medicine. The word "bezoar" (you say it like this: bē zōr) is thought to come from the Persian *pâdzahr*, which means "antidote," or "counter-poison." As far back as the seventh century, bezoars were used in the Muggle Islamic world. They were usually obtained from goats, but also from the guts of deer, camels, and cows. Before being used, the bezoar would be smashed up and ground into a powder. Then, it would either be gulped down, or taken with hot water in the form of a drink like tea. Muggles really believed in the power of the bezoar. They even made it into a bandage, and used it as a remedy for fever and diseases like epilepsy or leprosy.

Slowly, over the centuries, the bezoar became known to Muggle doctors in Europe. In the 1300s in Europe around fifty million people perished in the black death. This was a plague that swept through Europe, and also parts of Asia and Africa. So the idea of the bezoar, a powerful medicine, was very appealing to the suffering Muggle Europeans. King Edward IV of England believed his recovery from a wound was due to his Muggle doctor using a bezoar.

Bezoars as Gems

The fame and fortune of bezoars soon rocketed. They even appeared among lists of gems. For example, there was a price list made by a German Muggle chemist in 1757. On the list he had sapphires, emeralds, rubies, and other precious gems. But the real pick of the precious list was the bezoar. And its value was fifty times that of the value of emeralds!

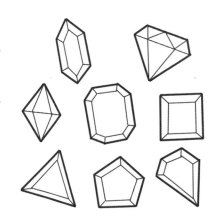

A bezoar would also be worn as an amulet. Amulets were objects that Muggles wore, often around their necks. They were believed to protect the Muggle from evil, diseases, or just plain unhappiness. If the bezoar wasn't worn around the neck, it was carried in jeweled boxes. Queen Elizabeth I of England, whose reign was at the time of Shakespeare, had several bezoars set in rings. They later became part of the crown jewels of the realm.

Muggle fraudsters even made fake or bogus bezoars. An English goldsmith was taken to court for making and selling worthless fakes in the early 1600s. The price he expected other Muggles to pay for his fake bezoar was a cool one hundred British Muggle pounds, or around $40,000 in today's money! And in 1714, a Fellow of the Royal College of Surgeons in London was driven mad about bizarre bezoar claims. At that time, a local chemist claimed he stocked five hundred ounces of bezoar in his shop. But the surgeon smelled a rat when he calculated that the chemist's stock of bezoars would mean he would have to have slaughtered about fifty thousand goats to get that weight of bezoars!

Does the Muggle bezoar really work as an antidote? To answer that question, consider this tale. King Charles IX of France was given a bezoar as a gift. Unlike his countryman Napoleon, Charles was pleased. So the King called up his royal doctor, Ambroise Paré. The King wanted to know if the stone really did have the power to protect His Majesty against all possible poisons. Rubbish! said the royal doctor. No two toxins are exactly the same, he replied, so no single stone could have the power to be an antidote for all.

Fine, says the king, then we shall test it to find the truth. So the king now called up a convicted criminal. This criminal had been sentenced to hanging, and was soon due to die. But a new choice was given to him. Eat a deadly poison, and then the bezoar. If you are cured, you go free. The criminal took his chance of freedom. He gulped down a poison prepared by the royal chemist, hurriedly followed by bolting down the bezoar. Lo and behold, he died. In agony. A few hours later. Meanwhile, is that the sizzling sound of a stone the doctor can hear? Has the king thrown the so-called cure-all bezoar onto the fire?

DEVIL'S SNARE: WHAT ARE THE REAL-LIFE FLESH-EATING PLANTS?

Herbology is one of the many fascinating topics that students study at Hogwarts. Herbology is all about magical plants and fungi. Although it's sometimes overlooked, Professor Sprout's lessons help Harry, Ron, and Hermione out of many sticky situations during their time at the Castle.

One of the deadliest of the plants that Harry encounters, both in and outside the Herbology classroom, is Devil's Snare. In the Golden Trio's

Voldemort-busting adventure through the trapdoor, Devil's Snare is one of many trials that they have to beat to reach the Sorcerer's Stone.

Devil's Snare has the amazing ability to grip its prey. And, as Ron and Harry discover, the more you struggle, the tighter it grips and squeezes. Later in the story series, Devil's Snare features as a deadly weapon more than once. During the Battle of Hogwarts, Neville Longbottom and Professor Sprout use Devil's Snare in positions around the grounds of Hogwarts to try to stop the Giants and Death Eaters from invading the Castle.

In another sinister scene, Devil's Snare is smuggled into St Mungo's Hospital for Magical Maladies and Injuries. Once in the hospital, it's used as a method of assassination. A potted Devil's Snare is delivered to a patient in a coma, Broderick Bode. The Death Eater responsible, Walden Macnair, was able to sneak the plant past the Healers, who mistake it for a Christmas gift. And the plant strangles Bode to death before anyone realizes what's happening.

Luckily for Harry and Ron, there's an easy way to escape Devil's Snare. The harder you struggle against its grip, the faster it starts to choke you. But if you keep still, you can trick the Snare into relaxing its grip on you. Thanks to Professor Sprout's Herbology class, Hermione is able to escape its clutches and then manages to save a very panicked Ron by conjuring fire to make its tentacles recoil.

The fast-moving vines of the Devil's Snare are very impressive. And yet there are fascinating and deadly plants in Muggle botany.

Bladderwort—Not So Innocent

Like Devil's Snare at St Mungo's, this plant at first seems small and innocent. But given its very Potterish name, a Muggle might guess there's also something weird about bladderwort. Even though it's covered with pretty flowers, it's also pretty good at capturing prey. The plant has the name bladderwort because it has bladder-like traps, which it uses to trap small creatures. Bladderworts live in both fresh water and wet soil, on land or in water, and in most places across the planet, apart from Antarctica.

Bladderwort acts pretty swiftly. It can take just ten thousandths of a second for its trap to spring. In water, its trapdoor is triggered, and the prey, along with the surrounding water, is sucked into the bladder. Muggles believe the bladder traps are one of the most sophisticated in the plant kingdom. Thankfully, its prey is relatively small fry. The water-based species, common bladderwort, has bladders that feed on prey such as water fleas, mosquitos, and young tadpoles. By grabbing them by the tail, bladderwort gobbles up tadpoles and mosquitos by eating them, bit by bit.

The Venus Flytrap—The Classic

Venus flytrap is the classic flesh-eating plant of the Muggle world. And, with moving leaves that close around its prey, the Venus flytrap makes a grasping trap, which is very like the sinister clutches of the magical Devil's Snare.

The Venus flytrap is a miracle of nature. Muggles don't normally think of plants that move. But the flytrap can catch insects by moving its toothed leaves. They snap shut when the plant is triggered by prey touching the tiny hairs on the inner surface of the leaf.

The way the Venus flytrap works is quite complex and clever. Imagine a spider, stupid enough to be clambering across the inside of a Venus flytrap leaf. If the arachnid triggers one of the tiny hairs on the inside surface of the leaf, the trap starts to close. It snaps shut when it feels a second contact within about twenty seconds of the first one. This means that the Flytrap doesn't waste energy by trapping things that it can't eat. A Venus flytrap will only begin digesting after five such triggers, to make sure it's caught a live bug worthy of chomping.

And here's another cool thing the Venus flytrap can do. The speed of the snap shut depends on the amount of light, the size of prey, and other conditions the plant finds itself in. The speed with which the trap shuts tells Muggles whether the plant is healthy, even if the same can't be said for its prey, which includes beetles, spiders, and other crawling arthropods.

The Venus flytrap boasts some very famous fans. The founder of geographical botany, John Dalton Hooker, was director of the Royal Botanic Gardens, at Kew in London. He shared an interest in carnivorous plants with his closest and most famous friend, Charles Darwin, who called the Venus flytrap "one of the most wonderful plants in the world."

The Giant Hogweed—Poisoned by Touch Alone

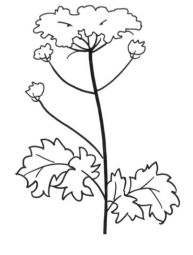

Giant hogweed is the plant of nightmares. Many plants prove poisonous if you eat them. But the giant hogweed, which grows up to eight feet tall, can poison you by touch alone. Looking like something from an alien planet, hogweed poisons with the help of an extraterrestrial body—the sun! As hogweed is sensitive to sunlight, it oozes a thick sap that coats human skin when touched. At once, the sap reacts with the sun and starts a chemical reaction that burns through your flesh. Ouch! This contact can lead to massive, purple lesions on the skin. What's worse is the lesions may last for years! And what's even worse than that is that a tiny amount of sap can cause permanent blindness if it touches your eye. Hardly surprising that giant hogweed plants are public enemy number one for Muggle plant-control departments.

DO REAL-LIFE
LOVE POTIONS WORK?

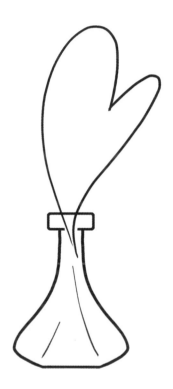

Is there a chemistry of love? There surely was in the wizard world. In the Harry Potter stories, love potions were brews of infatuation. In other words, if you drank a love potion, you became obsessed with the person who gave you the drink. Love potions were not only very powerful, they were also highly dangerous. The most powerful of these potions was Amortentia. It had a pearly look, and steam seemed to spiral off the top of the potion while it was being brewed.

Love potions were banned at Hogwarts. But witches and wizards still used them to try to win the hearts of others. Even Ron's mom, Molly Weasley, said she had once brewed a love potion when she was a young witch at Hogwarts. The usual practice was to hide a love potion in food or drink, so the victim would know no better.

Getting potions into Hogwarts was tough. The Weasley shop, Wizard Wheezes, started selling a series of love potions as part of its WonderWitch promotion. And when Hogwarts caretaker Argus Filch banned all their products from the school, Fred and George Weasley instead shipped in potions disguised as perfumes and cough syrups. So the young witches and wizards of Hogwarts traded in love potions, despite their owls being searched.

Now, Muggles have toyed with the idea of love potions for hundreds of years. Foods like chocolate, avocado, oysters, and honey have all been thought to be great for love. But what about Muggle love potions? And what's the chance they might actually work?

Muggle Mixtures

Muggles have also been dreaming up love potions for a long time. And some Muggles even think that love potions could soon become a reality. And here's the reason why. When Muggles fall in love, the effect on their brains is unique. Chemicals are set free in the Muggle brain that help build the bond of love. The chemicals cause the Muggles to think that their partner is someone who should stick around, someone they should feel bonded to.

Muggles also miss their partners' smell. When Muggle lovers are apart, their bodies release a chemical called CPH that shows the Muggle body is under stress and missing their partner. So some Muggle chemists think a real love potion could be created from a mixture of these chemicals, including CPH. A proper love potion won't be available at your chemist just yet.

But brain science is developing swiftly. Muggles know far more about the brain than they used to. They're better at understanding the brain, and they're better at modeling the Muggle brain's network of links. So that means, within ten years or so, Muggles might be able to brew what Professor Snape might call an elixir of love. Would you take the potion?

DO MUGGLE SPIES HAVE THEIR OWN VERITASERUM POTION?

"It is Veritaserum—a Truth Poison so powerful that
three drops would have you spilling your innermost
secrets for this entire class to hear."
—J. K. Rowling, *Harry Potter and the Goblet of Fire* (2000)

Three things, they say, cannot be hidden for long: the sun, the moon, and the truth. Muggles often say that the truth is rarely pure, and never simple. And yet in the Harry Potter stories, they even tried bottling pure truth! Veritaserum was a magical truth serum. It was strong and forced the drinker of the serum to answer truthfully any questions they were asked. The name Veritaserum is a word which comes from the Latin *veritas*, meaning "truth," and the Latin *serum*, meaning "liquid" or "fluid."

The Ministry of Magic was very strict about the way in which Veritaserum could be used. But there were also ways to keep the serum from working, such as swiftly swallowing an antidote! Potions masters like Professor Snape would say that Veritaserum had a complex chemistry. Chemistry, you may remember, is the study of the Muggle "magic" of how substances are made and the ways in which they react, or combine. When made carefully, the Veritaserum was clear, colorless, and odorless, which meant the serum looked just like water! Very sneaky. Severus Snape said that the serum needed to brew for a full phase of the moon before use.

Because it looked like water, Veritaserum was easily hidden by mixing with most drinks. Three drops was enough to make the drinker divulge their "innermost secrets." So the serum worked its magic on the body and mind of the drinker, making them tell the truth to any question asked. All according, of course, to whatever the drinker thought was true. Have Muggle spies ever used something from their own chemistry to make Muggles spill their innermost secrets?

Truth Serums: Scopolamine

Muggles have dreamed for many years about some kind of truth super-serum. And a number of chemicals have been thought to relax a Muggle so that they can't help but reveal the truth. The first of these chemical serums was scopolamine. Scopolamine is pronounced like this: "skow-po-luh-meen." Normally, it's used by Muggles to treat car sickness and nausea after surgery.

But about a hundred years ago, a Muggle doctor in Dallas called Robert House made a new discovery about scopolamine. He learned that with scopolamine in their systems, suspects "cannot create a lie . . . and there is no power to think or reason." The idea of a "truth drug" was launched upon the Muggle world. Doctor House wrote a lot about scopolamine in the 1920s. And he became known as the "father of truth serum." Doctor House and the drug became so famous that the very threat of using scopolamine was enough to get suspects to confess! But there were problems with the serum. The other side effects of the drug included hallucinations, headache, a rapid heartbeat, and blurred vision. And all this was enough to distract the suspect from the point of their truth-telling interview.

Truth Serums: Sodium Thiopental

Another Muggle "truth serum" is sodium thiopental. It was first made in the 1930s. It's an anesthetic, which means that sodium thiopental is one of a group of drugs used to produce better sleep. It works by slowing down the speed of "messages" that travel through the Muggle brain and body. The more sodium thiopental there is in the Muggle, the more the speed of thinking slows down.

So the Muggle who has been given sodium thiopental becomes very chatty. And, when the drug has worn off, they quite forget what they had been saying and what they might have confessed! But Muggles also found that, when you take the drug, you may be more likely to tell people what you think they want to hear, rather than the truth itself!

Research has found that the drug will no doubt make you more inclined to talk and that when under its influence, you are also very suggestible. And that's because the drug is interfering with your higher centers, such as your cortex, where lots of decision making occurs. But there's also a worrying risk you will say whatever your interrogator wants to hear, rather than the truth. And so a Muggle magic brew of a truth serum is not as simple as the truth potions in Harry Potter. At least, not without the weird side effects!

WILL MUGGLES EVOLVE MENTAL POWERS LIKE SNAPE?

"Used properly, the power of Occlumency will help shield you from access or influence. In these lessons I will attempt to penetrate your mind. You will attempt to resist. Prepare yourself! Legilimens!"
—Snape during Harry Potter's Occlumency lesson, J. K. Rowling, *Harry Potter and the Order of the Phoenix* (2003)

According to Professor Severus Snape, the human mind is not a book. It can't just be unlocked and "read" with ease. And the thoughts of wizards are not "etched on the inside of skulls." Instead, according to Snape, the mind is like an onion. It is a complicated organ of layers within layers. And yet, the wizards and witches who had mastered certain magical powers could still delve into the minds of their victims.

In the Harry Potter world, the skill of magically passing through the many layers of a wizard's mind was called Legilimency. Witches and wizards known as Legilimens then had to be able to "read" what they found there. To Muggles, the skill might have been called "mind reading." The opposite of Legilimency was Occlumency. Wizards and witches used

Occlumency to shield their minds from the mind-reading powers of a Legilimens.

Voldemort used Legilimency. He could read minds wandlessly and without words and enter the minds of other wizards and witches. Voldemort was said to be the best Legilimens ever. Though the people who said this were his Death Eaters! Still, Harry made sure he mastered Occlumency to hide his mind from Voldemort.

The word Occlumency sounds a bit like the word "occult." The occult (from the Latin word *occultus*, which means hidden or secret) is "knowledge of the hidden." But occult also means "knowledge of the paranormal," which is kind of opposite to science, which is "knowledge of the measurable."

So what does science have to say about mind reading? And what are the chances of Muggles in the future being able to read minds?

Facts of the Mind

The nearest thing to mind reading at present on our planet is "shark sense." Sharks, and several other fishes, have an amazing ability to sense electricity. They use special organs inside their bodies to sense nerve impulses in other fishes and worms. Sharks do this as the worms and fishes are their prey, and they are hurriedly trying to escape from the shark by burying themselves in seabed sand, away from the predatory shark.

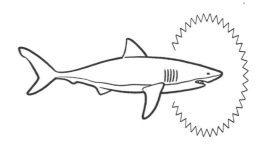

But the "reading" of thoughts, straight from brain to brain, would need a Muggle who could read electromagnetic signals being sent out by another Muggle brain. The electromagnetic spectrum is the complete range of radiation, from the longest radio waves to the shortest gamma waves. And even if this special Muggle could find a channel of "chatter" to read the other brain, the two Muggle minds would need to be matching. In other words, the bits of the brain in one Muggle would need to have the exact same purpose as the bits of the brain in the other Muggle whose mind they were reading.

We know this is not the case for Muggle brains. Not even in identical Muggle twins. Even twins have slightly different lives in their early years. And these differences program each Muggle brain with different links and with all sorts of different meanings compared to other Muggles, even their twin. So, an idea like "quidditch" will have different brain meanings from one Muggle to another.

The same would go for wizards and witches, too. The different experiences of a lifetime would mean very different brains. And so matching thoughts and minds would make it hard for messages to pass from one wizard or witch to another. The minds of wizard-kind would be as different from one another as Muggle minds are.

For Muggles, science and tech might come to the mind-reading rescue. In the future, we might be able to develop a computer technology in which the Muggle brain is linked to computer systems. A modem, for example, such as those used by computers to link to the

Internet. If you put a modem in a Muggle brain, it might be possible to send messages to another device, planted in another Muggle head. This second device would then relay the message to the other Muggle who had a modem in his head. Ouch. But, to those who knew no better, it might look like Muggle mind reading!

COULD NATURE MAKE ITS OWN FLUFFY?

History has many hellhounds. These supernatural dogs from folklore are often guardians of an underworld, the supernatural, or the realm of the dead. And sometimes, even if their name is Fluffy, they guard the Sorcerer's Stone at Hogwarts Castle.

Fluffy was bought by Hagrid from a "Greek chappie" at the Leaky Cauldron. Fluffy was a huge and vicious three-headed dog whose greatest weakness was to fall fast asleep at the first sound of music. Harry, Ron, and Hermione first met Fluffy in the forbidden area on the third floor of the Castle. Hermione, as sharp as ever, noticed that like most other hellhounds in history, Fluffy was guarding something. He was standing on a trapdoor, which the three students later figured out was the way to the Sorcerer's Stone.

When the three met Fluffy once more, Harry had brought along a flute, so that it could be played and help lull Fluffy asleep. Once the Stone was destroyed, and Fluffy's duties done, Hagrid took Fluffy to the Forbidden Forest and set him free. Soon after, Dumbledore sent Fluffy back to his native Greece. And yet the movie version of Fluffy appears to be a breed of English dog known as a Staffordshire Bull Terrier. To make the three heads look more "realistic," each was given its own personality—one "smart," one "alert," and one "sleepy."

But whether Fluffy was Greek or English, could nature make its own Fluffy?

Many-Headed Monsters

There have been lots of Muggle stories of many-headed monsters in history. Take the tale of that "Greek chappie" Heracles. He was faced with many labors, and one was to face up to a many-headed Hydra. Heracles saw that if you chopped off one of the beast's heads, it would just grow another! A multiheaded creature with re-growable body parts is a wonderful idea for a story. But from where do tales like Hydra's and Fluffy's come? Could the idea have come from nature itself?

For many years, Muggles have found real-life cases of many-headed creatures. In the 1940s, a two-headed pipefish embryo was called a "tiny monstrosity." More recently, Muggles have seen samples of two-headed creatures in their labs. Using modern science, Muggles have learned that nature allows for such creatures and that similar ancient cases could have led to the telling of the original tales. Ancient storytellers may have seen such freaky forms and put them into their stories.

Two-headed, and even three-headed, animals are sometimes found in the wild. And all sorts of animals might have more than one head. In recent years, a two-headed bull shark fetus was found in the Gulf of Mexico, and a double-headed dolphin washed up on a Turkish beach. Both are examples of what's known as "conjoined twins"—babies that develop from an egg that fails to divide after being made. Babies like this will often also have twin sets of some internal organs and even limbs.

The list of many-headed creatures includes beasts born millions of years ago. It includes not only snakes, turtles, and kittens, but also ancient monsters that Muggles have found in the fossil record. They think there are lots of ways in which a creature can have more than one head or face. And one big influence is genes. Remember that a gene is a part of the DNA in your body that controls the way you grow and the way you behave, which you inherit from your parents. All plants and animals have genes. They do different jobs.

There's one gene that has a big influence on how wide a creature's face becomes. It's known by Muggles as the Sonic Hedgehog gene, or SHH. The gene was given this name because a set of "hedgehog" (HH) genes can cause fruit flies to be born with spiky hairlike structures, and look like teeny hedgehogs!

If the SHH signal is strong when some creatures are growing, weird things can happen. The head can get so wide that you get two faces rather than one. We're some way to Fluffy, but not all the way there yet. The Sonic gene may make many faces, but not many heads. For a separate neck and head growing from the same body, a group of cells in the early egg would have to be working hard. Muggles are starting to learn why this happens, and one important factor seems to be temperature. For example, one Muggle found higher water temperatures was an influence on the birth of two-headed zebrafish!

So, in some ways, nature has already made its own Fluffy. Muggles still have much to learn about our planet's many-headed creatures. The trouble is, many-headed creatures don't survive for very long when they're born. That means the idea of multiheaded monsters is likely to have a long life in stories, even if they don't in nature!

WHERE AND WHEN MIGHT MUGGLES FIND DRAGONS?

"What's life without a few dragons?"
—J. K. Rowling, *Harry Potter and the Goblet of Fire* (2000)

The smooth scarlet scales of the Chinese Fireball. The yellow eyes and bronze horn of the Hungarian Horntail. The black spine of the Norwegian Ridgeback. And the copper-colored scales of the Peruvian Vipertooth. There are plenty of dragons to choose from in Harry Potter's world.

Even the motto of Hogwarts School was *Draco dormiens numquam titillandus*, or "Never tickle a sleeping dragon." And the Hogwarts gamekeeper, Rubeus Hagrid, truly adored dragons. For a short time, Hagrid cared for a Norwegian Ridgeback named Norbert. When Norbert turned out to be female, he was swiftly renamed Norberta!

In Harry's world, the stuff of dragons, such as their blood, was very valuable. The only problem was actually getting such samples. It needed over a dozen wizards or witches just to stun a dragon. Dragons were kept on special reserves around the world. This made it less likely that the dragons would be seen by Muggles, who believed them to be creatures of mere myth. Dragons could not be kept as pets, despite people like Hagrid trying to do so. And wizard zoologists who were experts in looking after dragons were known as dragonologists.

In the Muggle world, the dragons in myths and stories often have the traits and features of many other creatures. For example, dragons from India might have the head of an elephant. Those from the Middle East might have the traits of a lion, or a bird of prey. And the color of dragon bodies, from green, red, or black to the rarer yellow, blue, or white, is like an echo of the culture in which the dragon is imagined.

But, if a Muggle were looking for a dragon, where and when might they find one?

A History of Dragons

Dragons have been in Muggle stories for many centuries. You can still find dragons on the flags of some countries, such as Wales, Bhutan, and Malta. Dragons were also on the Chinese flag during the days of the Qing dynasty, hundreds of years ago, so dragon history is a long and ancient one.

Little is known of the time when and where the stories of dragons first began. But by the time of the ancient Greeks, tales were already being told of huge flying serpents. Long ago, dragons were thought to be sometimes kind, and sometimes downright dangerous, like other fantastic beasts. But tales of kindly dragons seemed to vanish in a puff of smoke. Dragons became one of the few creatures of fantasy that were not only powerful, but were also a worthy and awesome enemy to be slain. Dragons were now thought to have fiery breath.

In medieval times, the Dutch Muggle Hieronymus Bosch made a painting that showed fire-breathing dragons over the mouth of hell! If you were to look closely at the right panel of Bosch's *Garden of Earthly Delights* painting, done in the early 1500s, you might spot the odd dragon, flying high above the pits of hellfire. The Gates of Hell were often shown as the mouth of a monster, with smoke and flames belching out.

Here Be Dragons

Is there Muggle evidence of a link between dragons and real creatures? Maybe. The belief in dragons wasn't simply conjured out of thin Muggle air. There was evidence in the form of giant bones, which were unearthed in various parts of the world. For thousands of years, few Muggles knew what to make of them. But, in time, dragons became the guess of choice for those Muggles with no knowledge of dinosaurs.

The word "dragon" comes from the ancient Greek word *draconta*, which means "to watch." You can see why J. K. Rowling chose dragons to guard the mountains of gold at Gringotts. Muggles never seemed to wonder why a creature as powerful as a dragon might need coins to pay for anything! Maybe it was a reward for the brave adventurers who managed to kill the mighty beast and pick up the cash.

Today, few Muggles think that huge and fantastic fire-breathing dragons still lurk in some lost land. Or that they wait to be discovered as they fly about some uncharted skies, still unseen by Muggles. But, just a few centuries back, it was believed that dragons were finally discovered.

Sailors returning from Indonesia told tales of the Komodo dragon. Deadly and dangerous, the Komodo dragon can reach ten feet in length. Muggles wondered if the Komodo dragon might be a flightless cousin of more exotic beasts elsewhere on the planet. This new myth was helped by the belief that the bite of the Komodo dragon was deadly. Its very breath was poisonous. The myth lasted until 2013, when a team of Muggles from the University of Queensland found that the Komodo mouth was no fuller of poisonous bacteria than those of other carnivores.

So, the dragon is like a kind of chameleon of the Muggle imagination. Muggles have now shown that a huge collection of creatures has influenced the modern idea of a dragon. Traits and features of huge snakes and hydras, gargoyles and dragon-gods, as well as more weird beasts, such as basilisks, wyverns, and cockatrices, work their way into what we Muggles think a dragon might look like. Most Muggles will find it easy to imagine a dragon. But their ideas and descriptions of dragons vary hugely! Some Muggles might picture winged dragons; others plant them squarely on the ground. Some dragons are given voice, or breathe fire; others are made mute and smokeless. Some might be measured in mere yards; others span a measure in miles. And some dragons are pictured in a submarine world, while others are found only in caves on the highest hills.

So, if we Muggles are looking for fabulous creatures, draconian in sheer size and variety, our best bet would be to travel back to the days of the dinosaur, when they became the dominant beast on the planet, over 200 million years ago.

WHY WOULD PIGEONS, AND NOT OWLS, MAKE A WIZARD'S BEST FRIEND?

"Because owls are mostly nocturnal, with night vision and an innate hunting instinct, superstitions about their magical power have been associated with the darker side of witchcraft. . . . Shakespeare's use of the owl's shriek to signal the death of King Duncan in Macbeth shows how owls were seen as evil omens during the Renaissance. So, like the witches and wizards they serve so efficiently in the wizarding world, owls have been the subject of Muggle superstition. It's a pity: they run a very efficient postal service."
—J. K. Rowling, *Pottermore* (2019)

They ghost through the air on shadowy, moonlit nights. They make their muffled way, under skies of Bible-black, through the Castle's dark towers. And they glide on nameless winds, their haunting cry the only hint that they carry messages for Harry and the rest of the wizarding world.

Owls are as common in nature as they are in the magic world of Harry Potter stories. Owls are found across the planet, with over two hundred species of this solitary bird. Owls come out at night, are usually upright in posture, have fantastic vision, and have feathers that evolved for silent flight. Rarely do owls appear by day.

The Asian eagle-owl, the bird owned by the Malfoys, has a wingspan of over six feet. They can eat a variety of small creatures (the owls, not the Malfoys!), including foxes, herons, and even small dogs. The Malfoy bird makes us realize that some owls are indeed large and strong enough to carry parcels. Though they are certainly clever enough, owls have never been used to deliver a postal service.

Muggles have held owls in high regard since before the beginning of civilization. The Chauvet-Pont-d'Arc Cave in southern France contains the clear image of an owl etched into the rock. The owl is shown on the cave wall with its head seen from the front, but its body seen from the back. Even prehistoric Muggles were amazed by what seemed to be the owl's "supernatural" power to swivel its head in this way. Early Muggles may also have been fascinated by the owl's ability to see in the dark, such as the cave itself. The Chauvet cave owl painting is thought to be at least 30,000 years old. So it's been a long time that Muggles have thought owls had magical powers. Though Muggles have never used owls as messengers, nature has given us some other stunning options.

Arctic Terns

The Arctic tern is one bird that never seems to tire out. Lots of birds migrate, spending one part of the year in one place, then flying somewhere far away to spend the rest of the year there. But no birds do this migration, as it's called, as spectacularly as the Arctic tern. The tern has not one but two summers each year. That's because it migrates from the Arctic North at the "top of the world" to the Antarctic South at the "bottom of the world" for the summer. Then it returns along the same path, six months later! Recent Muggle studies say that's a yearly round trip of around 44,000 miles for terns nesting in Iceland, and an incredible 56,000 miles for terns nesting in the Netherlands!

Arctic terns are by far the longest migratory creatures in the entire animal kingdom. They also live quite long lives, with many reaching fifteen to thirty years of age, in some cases outliving many wild owls. And there are plenty of Arctic terns on the planet, with about one million birds across the world. But the Muggles have never tried the Arctic tern as a message carrier. The prize for nature's best dispatch rider goes to the pigeon.

Using the Columbine

Consider the humble pigeon. Pigeons, along with doves, belong to the bird family Columbidae. The family includes over three hundred species, and is probably the most common bird in the world. The species to which Muggles refer most as "pigeon" is the rock pigeon. Pigeon flights as long as one thousand miles have been recorded, and their average flying speed is about the speed of a car. Pigeons have a long history as carriers. The Muggle Egyptians and Persians first used pigeons to carry messages around three thousand years ago. And the

Republic of Genoa set up a system of pigeon watchtowers that ran along the Mediterranean Sea.

But how do pigeons know where to fly? Nobody knows for sure. Some Muggle studies say that pigeons have a kind of map and compass in their heads. This means they sometimes use the sun to figure out where they're going and, since the earth is like a big magnet, they may also use the earth's magnetic field to get them home. When they get close to where they're going, the theory supposes, they also use landmarks.

Muggles used pigeons as messengers in World War II. The pigeons were taken on Lancaster bombers, and the birds helped in the war effort as the British Royal Air Force Pigeon Corps! The idea was that if the pigeons were let out over the North Sea, on the way back from a bombing flight over Germany, the flight navigator would tie to the leg of the pigeon a map reference of where the plane last was, in case radio contact was broken. These pigeons saved thousands of lives.

War Heroes

Did the war pigeons use magnetism and landmarks to work out where they were? Maybe not. Some pigeons were released in the middle of the night, in freezing fog, one hundred miles from land, with no landmarks in sight. They still got home. The most outstanding of the pigeons were given medals by the British. The true hero list of pigeons has about five hundred examples of astonishing feats. Many were dropped out of planes in the middle of nowhere, often at night and in winter, but still got home the next morning.

To try and figure out how pigeons did this, Muggles went to work. Muggles blocked the pigeons' nostrils up with wax. Muggles tried to confuse the birds by placing the smell of turpentine on their beaks. Muggles figured the mysterious sense of the birds might be smell. So they even cut off the pigeons' sense of smell.

Though they had little success, the Muggles carried on with their weird experiments. They strapped magnets to the birds' wings. They even wound magnetic coils around the pigeons' heads. Even when the Muggles fitted the birds' eyes with frosted glass contact lenses, and released them over two hundred miles away from home, they still flocked down within a quarter of a mile of their loft! Even if the pigeons were let out on cloudy days, or if their body clocks had been shifted by six hours, or twelve hours, they still came home.

Every one of these Muggle experiments was to test to see if the pigeons had a body compass, or to see if they used landmarks on the ground below. One Muggle experiment even drugged the pigeons and placed them in rotating drums trying to confuse the pigeon's sense of direction, yet, on release, they flew straight home.

Home Ties

For over one hundred years, pigeons have remained something of a Muggle mystery. Famous Muggle scientist Charles Darwin had a pigeon theory. He said that pigeons might remember their journey out and repeat it on the way home. But the experiments during the war proved Darwin was wrong, which just goes to show even the most famous Muggle scientists can make mistakes.

And yet, there seems to be some connection between the pigeon and its home. As almost all past experiments tried moving the pigeons from their home, a new set of experiments moved their home instead. A mobile pigeon loft! The British Pigeon Corps used mobile lofts behind the front lines in World War I. Like the Night Bus in Harry Potter's magical world, the mobile pigeon lofts were fashioned out of London buses, converted especially for the purpose.

When the lofts were first moved, just a half a mile away, the pigeons seemed totally confused. Though they could see the slightly moved loft, they encircled the area, flying about the place where the loft used to be, for a few hours. Just as a wizard might be confused if he'd found his home had been moved one hundred yards down the street while he was away. Eventually, the bravest of the birds would try out the new loft location by simply diving in. After the loft had been moved several times, the rest of the pigeons returned home.

So the secret of the pigeon's fame as a message carrier remains a Muggle mystery. The pigeon seems the perfect bird for the wizarding world. Making their way with the latest wizard word, come hell or high water, from home, to Diagon Alley, and to a huge Hogwarts Loft in the Castle's West Tower.

WHY ARE DEATH EATER "PURE-BLOODS" WRONG ABOUT RACE?

In Harry's world, the term "pure-blood" was used by wizard families who said they had no Muggle, or nonmagic, blood in their family trees. The idea of the pure-blood was begun by Salazar Slytherin, one of the four founders of Hogwarts School of Witchcraft and Wizardry. Slytherin hated teaching Muggle-born students. His hatred led to an argument with his three fellow founders and his leaving the school.

So-called pure-blood wizard families thought they were superior to witches and wizards who had Muggles in their family trees. But "pure-bloods" were never what they seemed. Even though they claimed to have a purely magical heritage, in truth they did not. They were not "pure." They denied or lied about the Muggle-borns on their family trees. And yet they still tried to keep their bloodline "pure" by breeding only with other "pure-bloods." They also used the word "Mudbloods" to describe wizard families with Muggle-born ancestors. "Mudbloods" was a very nasty term in the wizarding world.

Faced with the fact of a changing world, "pure-bloods" also said that any witch or wizard who mixed with "Mudbloods" was a "blood traitor." But, of course, and as Muggle science would have told them, there was not a witch or wizard whose blood had not at some time mixed with that of Muggles. If there were no Muggles in wizarding family trees, wizard-kind would have died out long ago. The number of "pure-blood" families was dropping, and their blood type the least common in the magical world.

But what does science have to say about the views of "pure-blood" wizards and witches? What does nature reveal for the Death Eaters, whose leader denied he had a "filthy Muggle father"?

Breed Outside Your Local Pool

First up, it makes total sense for wizard-kind and Muggles to mate. Making families within a small circle can be downright dangerous. Most people have a few hidden genes that can cause deadly diseases. But it's not normally a problem. And that's because we carry two copies of each gene: one from each parent. So, as long as one of the two gene copies is fine, you don't usually get the disease. Bad genes kick in only if both parents pass it down to their offspring. And that would have happened more often when wizards were more closely related.

In fact, some wizards and witches might be dicing with danger. The more closely related a wizard and witch are, the more likely it is they share the same bad genes. In such cases, each child can have up to a 25 percent chance of getting the disease. This is the reason inbreeding, as it's called, is banned in many Muggle countries.

Let's look at two examples, one wizard and one Muggle.

"Pure-blood" wizarding families, such as Sirius Black's clan, married their cousins to keep their "pure-blood" status. They had nothing to do with any family members who married a "Mudblood." And yet wizarding families like theirs had problems—family members had violent tendencies, mental health issues, and even suffered from weaker magical powers.

The same was true in the old Muggle royal families of Europe. Inbreeding was a problem. The Habsburgs ruled large parts of Europe for many centuries. But after many marriages between first cousins, and even uncles and nieces, when King Charles II was born his inherited "bad genes" meant he had physical and mental issues. He couldn't have children, and so the Habsburg rule ended.

In 2015, a large Muggle study looked into this matter of breeding and inheritance. The study looked at the background and health of more than 350,000 people from about 100 communities across four continents of the Muggle world. It found that the children of parents who are more distantly related tend to be taller and smarter than others. They also found that Muggle height and Muggle brainpower is increasing, as a growing number of Muggles are marrying people from more distant parts of the Muggle world. This may also explain the increase in intelligence from one generation to the next, noticed throughout the twentieth century.

So, "pure-blood" wizards had it all wrong all along. It's "Mudbloods" who will inherit the earth!

PART IV
MAGICAL MELTING POT

PLATFORM 9¾: ARE THERE REAL HIDDEN RAILWAY STATIONS IN LONDON?

"It is said (though where the story originated I could not tell you; it is suspiciously vague) that King's Cross station was built either on the site of Boudicca's last battle (Boudicca was an ancient British Queen who led a rebellion against the Romans) or on the site of her tomb. Legend has it that her grave is situated somewhere in the region of platforms eight to ten. I did not know this when I gave the wizards' platform its number."
—J. K. Rowling, *Pottermore* (2019)

The mighty scarlet engine awaits. Billowing clouds cascade down onto its metal track. The steam engine is a stepping-stone to some magical far-off destination. All windows down, all pistons poised, all sense of being in a hurry gone, the Hogwarts Express will soon pull out. A fleeting appearance in a thousand neighborhoods, and later the Express will run where sky and water meet, where the Black Lake's level breadth begins. Later.

For now, the scarlet engine still sits on a platform that denies its own existence: Platform 9¾, King's Cross Station, London, England.

Magically hidden behind the barrier between Muggle platforms 9 and 10, Platform 9¾ is where students board the train for Hogwarts School of Witchcraft and Wizardry. A curious young witch or wizard might have wondered what other platforms lay between the whole-numbered platforms. Why stop at 9¾? Perhaps on platform 9½ there's a magical version of the Orient Express that waits to whisk passengers off to wizard-only villages in Europe. Or maybe on platform 9¼ there's a once-every-four-years special to the Quidditch World Cup.

The idea for platform 9¾ was conjured up during the 1850s, in the mind of the Minister for Magic, Evangeline Orpington. The Ministry of Magic had long thought about the ages-old problem of how to get hundreds of students to and from Hogwarts every year, without Muggles ever seeing them. The Ministry had bought the Hogwarts Express in the mid 1800s—a magnificent engine for its time. A railway station had then been built at Hogsmeade, knowing that the engine would one day soon pull into its platform.

But there was a problem for wizard-kind. How on earth do you build a railway station in the middle of London, under the noses of prying Muggles? Surely even Muggles would notice magic right in front of their very faces, even if they missed obvious magic most of the time. So a solution was struck: a magical platform would be hidden within the new Muggle-built King's Cross Station—a platform reachable by witches and wizards only.

This cunning idea, to hide a secret railway station in a busy metropolis, makes a Muggle wonder what other stations might be hidden beneath the streets of old London town.

Railway Revolution

In Britain, about 260 years ago, there began the Industrial Revolution, powered by steam. It was a time when Muggles began working more with machines in factories than by hand at home. And the Muggles who built the steam trains and railroads had a special place. They were like the shock troops of the Industrial Revolution. That's because railways opened up countries and continents to the business of making money. The railway lines spread across Britain and the rest of the world like the giant web of some machine monster. And, at the heart of this huge monster—like the pulsing heart of the business world—sat Victorian London. During the 1800s, London grew greatly. But this huge city had its problems. The growing population led to growing traffic.

Horse poop became a major problem! Old London town had around 11,000 cabs and several thousand omnibuses. Each vehicle used several horses, so the city used more than 50,000 horses for public transport. Now, each animal made between 15 and 35 pounds of poop per day. One Muggle from the time said, "How much pleasanter the streets of a great city would be if the horse was an extinct animal."

Muggles had various jobs to help keep the city clean. Sweepers helped clear paths through the poop, which was usually sludge in the wet weather of London, or a fine poop powder, blowing through the streets on the odd dry and breezy day. But the piles of poop attracted huge numbers of flies. One Muggle worked out that three billion flies hatched in horse poop every day in the city, with tens of thousands of deaths each year blamed on the poop.

The poop problems didn't end there. The horses also produced tens of thousands of gallons of pee every day. And they were amazingly noisy. Their iron shoes clopping down onto the old cobbled roads made conversation almost impossible on London's bustling streets. This whole horse traffic business made London far more dangerous then, when compared to modern motor traffic. In those days you were 75 percent more likely to die of traffic problems.

The problems didn't disappear when the horses died. The average working horse had a life expectancy of only three years. Scores died each day and, as dead horses were hard to move, street cleaners would wait days for the corpses to rot, so they could more easily be sawed into chunks.

Going Underground

So, London was a city that badly needed a traffic solution. And the train was the city's savior. By the middle of the 1800s, when J. K. Rowling says the Ministry of Magic had bought the Hogwarts Express, there were seven Muggle railway stations around London. And soon enough a brilliant Muggle idea was born: Why not build an underground railway that linked the City of London to these seven satellite stations?

These days, visitors to London know all about London's Underground. Its tube system was the world's first underground railway—a marvelous feat of Muggle engineering. Today, over one hundred miles of underground tracks carry more than four million passengers a day, one of the largest on the planet.

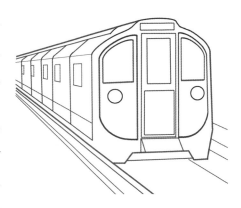

But, once in a while, "ghost" stations are unearthed. Stations hardly anyone knew were there. Muggle engineers in South London recently found the remains of a lost station, which shut over a hundred years ago. Its name was Southwark Park station. Since long-forgotten, Southwark Park was only open from 1902 until its catacombs were closed in March 1915. Muggle engineers found Southwark Park's abandoned creepy corridors and the eerie atmosphere of its heavily tiled ticket hall, where over a century ago Muggle passengers would have bought their tickets to travel underground as the throbbing city sat above. Southwark Park was one of several stations in the city that closed down around the start of World War I. At that time, trams and buses were becoming more popular, catering to commuters between the famous landmarks of London Bridge and Greenwich.

Explorers have snapped haunting photographs of other abandoned and long-forgotten London Underground stations. Lying deep below the city are empty platforms and derelict stations that snake for miles underground. Among them is the dusty Aldwych station, which closed in 1994 but has since been used as a set for movie and television productions including *Sherlock* and *V for Vendetta*.

But perhaps the best London Underground legend is the story of the secret government tunnels. During World War II, the number of telephone exchanges in London was very small, and they were too far apart.

For example, one of the main exchanges was in the City of London, and that's quite a long way from the War Office, the place where Britain's Army was run between the 1600s and 1964.

Running new phone lines aboveground wasn't a good idea. So the British government made a network of secret tunnels under London. Although the secret tunnels were just meant to be for the phone service, they could also be used as escape tunnels in emergencies such as gas attacks on the city. Many of the secrets about this tunnel network are locked away in dusty archives. But make a note in your schedule for the year 2026. That's when some of the secrets behind the tunnels will be released!

HOW COULD YOU MAKE A ROOM OF REQUIREMENT?

"According to Dobby, some folks knew it as the 'Come and Go Room', or the 'place where everything is hidden.' It wasn't long before we came to know the most mysterious place in Hogwarts as The Room of Requirement: a very useful nook as it turned out. . . . After all, the room only appeared when a person had real need of it – and always came equipped for the seeker's purpose. Any purpose . . ."
—J. K. Rowling, *Pottermore* (2019)

Situated on the seventh floor of Hogwarts Castle was the most remarkable of rooms. The room had a secret entrance near a tapestry that showed Barnabas the Barmy trying to teach trolls the basics of ballet. The Room of Requirement, as it was known, was both there and gone at the same time! Only a few visitors to that corridor knew the way to unlock the Room. You had to walk past it three times, thinking about what it was you most required. Only then would the magic door appear.

The Room was believed to be intelligent, up to a point. This belief was based on the fact that the Room turned itself into whatever the witch or wizard needed it to be at that particular moment in time. Though, of course, there were limits. It was also thought that the Room was unplottable. It didn't show on the Marauder's Map, nor did the Room's inhabitants. Although this could simply be because the map's makers never found the Room to plot it in the first place!

Witch or wizard users of the Room were told to be very exact but secretive about what they required the Room for. Those who didn't could quite easily find that other wizards could enter the Room and see what they were up to, if they knew how the Room was being used.

We first met the Room of Requirement when Dumbledore told Harry that he found a room full of chamber pots when he needed to go pee. Sadly, Dumbledore was never able to repeat this success. He never found the room again, like many other wizards who once happened upon the Room.

The Room of Requirement wasn't the only clever use of space in the Harry Potter stories, of course. There was also Hermione's beaded handbag. This was a bit like the carpetbag belonging to Mary Poppins. Hermione had placed an Undetectable Extension Charm on the handbag, in which she was able to keep all manner of objects. Some were much bigger than the bag appeared to be, especially during the hunt for Voldemort's Horcruxes.

Then there was the Weasleys' tent. It might look like a two-person pitch at first glance. But, when you entered, you found a fully furnished canvas palace, complete with dining table, kitchen, bathroom, and bedrooms. It was so impressive and so clever in its use of space that Harry declared, "I love magic!"

But how might Muggles be able to pull off the "bigger on the inside" technology of Hermione's handbag, the Weasleys' tent, and especially the Room of Requirement?

Muggle Theories of Gravity

One possible way is using gravity. About two thousand years ago the ancient Greek Muggle known as Aristotle had explained the way objects fall to the ground by saying it was simply their natural resting place. And the natural resting place for solid "earthy" bodies like Muggles was the center of the earth. Aristotle said the center of the earth was the center of the entire universe! And he even said that if you moved the earth, there would still be a point in space that was this center.

Fast-forward over two thousand years to a German Muggle genius called Albert Einstein. Einstein was the Muggle who came up with our modern idea of gravity, of why things fall to the ground. Einstein said that gravity is really a warp of space and time. In other words, massive things like planets and people bend space. So the matter of a body like the planet Earth will bend the space around it. And the more mass you have in one spot, the more that spot gets bent.

You can try experimenting with this idea quite easily, without even leaving your bed. Imagine space is like the surface of your comforter. At least, like your comforter when the bed is made, not crumpled up in a heap, as it normally is first thing in the morning. Okay, on this tidy, flat comforter you plonk a planet. Well, not an actual planet, but a tiny version of a planet: a soccer ball. Better still, a bowling ball, if you have one at hand in your bedroom!

The thing is this: the more massive the ball, the bigger the dip you make when you plonk your "planet." Not only that, but that dip around the ball seems to pull stuff nearby toward it. If you roll some smaller balls across the bed, you'll see this happen.

Now if you think of your balls as planets, and the comforter as the fabric of space, you can see just what Einstein was carrying on about. That's how gravity works: mass bends space. Also, the next time you get bad press for lazing about in bed, you can always suggest you're simply contemplating Einstein's theory of gravity. It might work!

The Muggle Use of Space

So, the best Muggle theory of gravity is the idea that gravity is a bending of space and time. Muggles like Einstein also think that an object that is free to move through space will move along the shortest path possible.

Now, if Muggles made a Room of Requirement, this is what they could do. They could make a room out of the right kind of material. Then, they could use all this gravity-bending to build a "bubble" that's bigger on the inside than out. The material they would use would be a very exotic type of matter, but hey, this creative use of space was never going to be easy.

Imagine one of the tiniest spiders from the Forbidden Forest, crawling along a flat upright wall. The square of the vertical wall has within it a bubble, which is kind of balloon-shaped. The narrow opening in the wall acts as a "throat," which opens out into a much bigger area. And if you scale this figure up into 3-D, it's roughly similar to the Room of Requirement (though the Weasleys' tent and Hermione's handbag may prove to be more of a challenge!). Another problem is that the material you'd need to use would be "exotic matter." It's very weird stuff. It's so weird, in fact, that if you pumped your car tires with it, they'd get flatter!

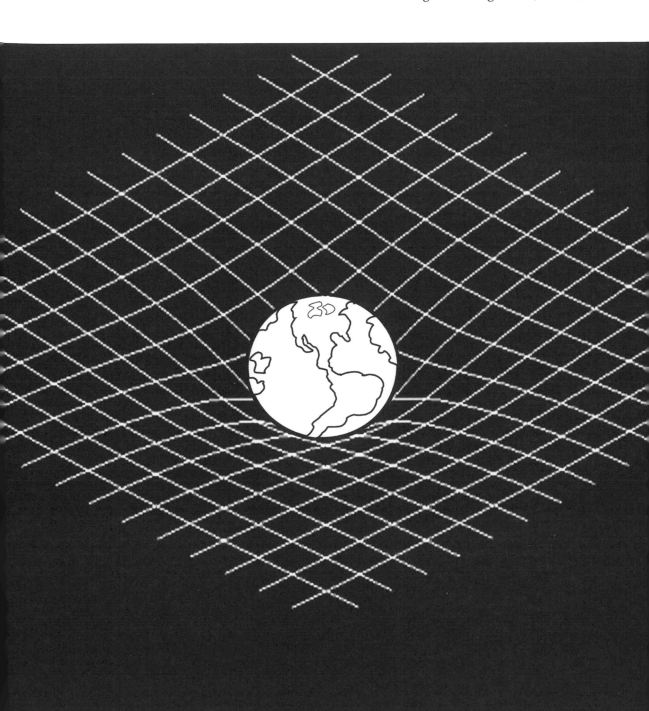

ARE FORCE FIELDS THE MUGGLE VERSION OF SHIELD CHARMS?

"Protego Fact File. TYPE: Charm. PURPOSE:
To cast a shield to protect a wizard.
THE EFFECT IT HAS ON THE RECIPIENT:
Protects the caster with an invisible shield."
—J. K. Rowling, *Pottermore* (2019)

Picture the scene. Hogwarts Castle is under siege from all manner of Death Eaters and dark and dangerous creatures. In a courtyard of the Castle, and under cover of darkness, Professor McGonagall declares, "Hogwarts is Threatened! Man the boundaries and protect us! Do your duty to our school!" Countless Castle statues and gargoyles thunder past, heading toward the viaduct—the position of the invading forces of darkness—all to McGonagall's obvious delight, "I've always wanted to use that spell."

A few yards away, Professor Flitwick waves his wand aloft and the summoning begins, "*Protego Maxima. Fianto Duri. Repello Inimicum.*" As other witches and wizards join with Flitwick, they glimpse a disturbance in the dark skies above the Castle. Together they conjure a magical shield, growing ever outward, as it bubbles and blooms over the Castle grounds, and, far below, the statues and gargoyles march along the viaduct and take their posts along the perimeter.

Flitwick had conjured up a Shield Charm on the Castle. Protego Maxima was a strong version of a Shield Charm which, when cast together with Fianto Duri and Repello Inimicum raised an almost unbreakable magical wall of defense. And that's how a Shield Charm (Protego) works. They create magical barriers to stop or block objects and spells. Shield Charms work to protect a person or a place. When Shield Charms are done well, other spells will just bounce off them as soon as they hit the Shield. Shield Charms seem so easily summoned in magic. But could Muggle technology conjure up something similar?

Nature's Force Fields

Recently, Muggle scientists found an invisible shield, 7,200 miles up above the earth. Now this natural shield really does help repel "dark" forces. The shield blocks "killer electrons," which are extremely small pieces of matter. Why are they "killer"? Because if it were not for the shield, the electrons would be free to bombard our planet. The thing is, these "killer electrons" can whiz around the world at the speed of light. They spook astronauts, fry satellites, and even wreck spacecraft. And, if they hit Earth on a huge scale, they could take out power grids, change the climate, and send cancer rates rocketing to an all-time high.

Muggles don't yet know how the shield works. Sure, Muggles know the shield is there. They can tell because of the effects it has on nature. The rest remains a mystery. But there is no doubt this real-life shield is quite like the Shield Charms at Hogwarts. The only difference is that rather than repelling Death Eaters, this invisible shield blocks high-speed electrons.

Thousands of miles above the earth sit invisible shields. They're like doughnut-shaped rings in the earth's atmosphere. They're full of high-energy particles and are held in place because our planet is like a big magnet. But they also block the ultrafast electrons from diving down deeper toward the earth.

Muggles think that one of these rings is like a glass wall in space, a bit like that bubble in the dark skies above Hogwarts. At first, Muggles were worried that the high-speed electrons, which are looping about the world at speeds greater than 100,000 miles per second, would bomb down into our upper atmosphere. But the "glass wall" stops the electrons before they get that far. If the Muggle science teams can figure out how the glass wall works, they may be able to mimic its magic and make a Muggle-made barrier that does the same!

WILL MUGGLES EVER HAVE ARITHMANCY?

Some might say Hermione Granger simply couldn't make her mind up about the future. She hated the school subject of Divination. Divination was the art of divining, or foretelling, future events by various tools and rituals. But she also said that Arithmancy was her favorite. Arithmancy was also a magical subject that studied the future. The difference between Arithmancy and Divination was that Arithmancy was a more exact and mathematical way of predicting the future. So the very sensible Hermione preferred it (one of her many complaints about Divination was that it seemed to be "a lot of guesswork").

Arithmancy was a subject all about the magical properties of numbers. So Arithmancy has something in common with the Muggle topic of numerology, where Muggles place their faith in number patterns and draw weird ideas from them. Arithmancy was only offered from the third year at Hogwarts.

Wizards and witches who practiced Arithmancy were called Arithmancers. Among the most famous wizard Arithmancers was Bartemius Crouch Jr. Crouch was the Death Eater who made Voldemort's return inevitable. Hermione also became a famous Arithmancer. She was a high-ranking official in the Department of Magical Law Enforcement.

So it looks like Harry did a spot of fortune-telling himself. He'd bought Hermione a copy of the book *New Theory of Numerology* for Christmas while they were still in school!

But can Muggles really use numbers to predict the future?

The Dark Archives

Muggles have a new subject in which they study numbers in society. The subject is called cliodynamics, as it's named after Clio, the Greek goddess of history. Muggles use cliodynamics to look for patterns in history, which can then be used to map out the future. One of the big questions Muggles aim to answer is "Why do civilizations collapse?"

The Muggle study of cliodynamics uses something mysteriously known as the dark archives. These archives are not as mysterious as they sound. They are data banks from the distant past, including documents from history that have only recently been put online. These data could be number data, or old newspapers and public records that have now been digitized, which just means they have been changed into a format that can be used with a computer.

The job of the Muggles using cliodynamics is this. They look through the dark archives and make predictions about the future based on the data banks. And Muggles have found some interesting patterns. The patterns apply to many civilizations, including the old Chinese dynasties, ancient Rome, medieval England, France, Russia, and the United States. The records clearly show one-hundred-year waves of uncertainty. And, on top of these waves, there's another fifty-year cycle of widespread trouble. China seems to be the only country that has managed in the past to avoid the fifty-year cycle of trouble.

The Muggles have blamed the cycles of uncertainty and trouble on the gap between rich people and poor people. Over a period of time, the gap between rich and poor creeps up, decade after decade. Until, that is, a breaking point is reached. Muggles in power then try to do something about the gap, but it is often too little, too late. And, even if something is done to lessen the gap, over time the gap gets bigger again, and the whole cycle starts again. A good example of this would be a lesson from history. The gap between rich and poor got so big in France that in 1789 the French Revolution happened. But Britain in the early 1800s was able to avoid a revolution by making changes that made things ever so slightly better for poor people.

So, much has been made by Muggles of their dark archives. Cliodynamics shows that much value can be found in historical records. Muggles never knew they had such treasure, which can possibly predict their future. So now, the Muggle world is taking a closer look. Muggle historians are starting to work with Muggle mathematicians to find out how our future may soon be predicted from our past.

COULD MUGGLES MASTER THE MEMORY TRANSFER OF A PENSIEVE?

The legend was this: the Pensieve was older than Hogwarts itself. The founders of the school were said to have discovered the Pensieve half buried in the ground. It was made of an ancient stone and carved with a strange sort of runes, which are letters of an ancient alphabet cut into stone or wood. The discovery meant that the Pensieve was made before the founding of Hogwarts, and was also said to be one of the reasons the school was set in such a remote place.

The Pensieve was used to store and sort memories. It looked just like a shallow stone basin. It was inlaid with carvings of runes and strange symbols. And it sat filled with a silvery substance, a bit like the metal mercury, and yet cloudlike. The witches and wizards who owned a Pensieve would use a wand to take a wispy form of their memories from their mind and place it in the silvery substance of the Pensieve.

A Pensieve held all the collected memories of the witches and wizards who had placed their thoughts into it. An impressive line of Hogwarts headmasters and headmistresses left behind their legacy, in the form of memory. This meant that any headmaster and headmistress could use a Pensieve as a kind of library of memories. We can assume that

Dumbledore added his memories to the mix, including his knowledge about the rise and fall of Voldemort. Dumbledore once said that he found the Pensieve very valuable in sorting through the mind, spotting links and patterns that might otherwise be missed.

The word "Pensieve" is a combination of the words "pensive" and "sieve." To sieve is to sort, or separate. And "pensive" means "to ponder," and also means "thoughtful" or "reflective." So together you can see that "Pensieve" means just what Dumbledore used it for—a magical relic that allows the sorting of thoughts and memories.

But witches and wizards had to be careful when they were using the Pensieve. As we saw when Dumbledore used Harry as wizard witness to past events, memories can be tricky. And this was especially true when the memory was highly intimate and personal. So the Pensieve was open to abuse. Most Pensieves were entombed with their owners, along with the memories they held. Some witches and wizards passed on their Pensieve and memories to other witches and wizards, as was the case with the Hogwarts Pensieve.

Imagine being able to sort your dreams and memories in real life! We might wonder what progress has been made in Muggle memory transfer. Will Muggles someday develop the tech that transfers memory like a Pensieve?

Shakespeare in a Syringe

In the world of Muggle science, between the late 1950s and the mid-1970s, it started to look like memory editing might actually be possible. Our tale begins with the transfer of memory in animals. At the time, Muggles thought memories were stored in chemicals, which could be moved from creature to creature. The research excited Muggles because if memories really were programmed into chemicals, what else might be possible?

Kindergarten kids could master their multiplication tables by simply swallowing a pill. College students could become fluent in a foreign language by having it inserted under their skin. And actors could memorize the complete works of Shakespeare by having Shakespeare's works injected into their bloodstreams! (My dad used to call William Shakespeare, "Billy Waggle-Dagger." Do you get the joke?)

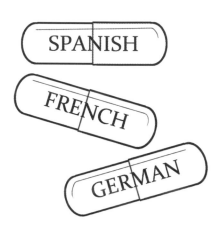

The Muggle memory engineering began well. The Muggle scientists thought they had taken memories out of the brain of one animal and placed it in another. Let's imagine the first creature had been trained in some task. After memory transfer, it seemed that the second creature would know how to perform the same task, but with far less training. The second creature maybe had a head start advantage, based on the memory "edit."

It all began with worms. The first tests were done on flatworms. They were trained to scrunch up their bodies in reaction to light. This is what happened: the Muggle scientists would shine a light on the worms as they made their way across the bottom of a shallow water tank. At the same time, the Muggles would give the worms a mild electric shock. So, in time, the worms would learn to associate the light with the shock. Eventually, the worms would scrunch up their bodies whenever the light was shone, whether or not there was also an electric shock. Worms that scrunched in reaction to light alone were called "expert" worms. Muggles were then able to show that "novice" worms, who had no experience of the experiments, would also scrunch up their bodies to light alone if they had some tissue transplanted into them from "expert" worms. They were getting a memory "edit," and it seemed to work!

And yet Muggles are curious creatures. After decades of work on the worm experiments, a very important Muggle scientist decided it was all nonsense. So, Muggle science simply didn't follow the story to the end. There are no reports that prove the idea of memory transfer is wrong. And many of the results have never been explained. Memory transfer was never disproved. Muggle scientists simply found another game to play. Who knows, maybe one day they'll change their minds again!

CAN MUGGLES DEVELOP THEIR OWN FORM OF TELEPORTATION?

"Harry felt Dumbledore's arm twist away from him and re-doubled his grip: the next thing he knew everything went black; he was pressed very hard from all directions; he could not breathe, there were iron bands tightening around his chest; his eyeballs were being forced back into his head; his ear-drums were being pushed deeper into his skull."
—J. K. Rowling, *Harry Potter and the Half-Blood Prince* (2005)

Witches and wizards pop up in the weirdest places, don't they? One moment they're contemplating cauldrons in Diagon Alley, and the next moment they're sipping butterbeer in The Hog's Head. But then, getting about in the wizarding world was easy. There were so many instant travel options, such as brooms, Floo Powder, and portkeys.

Maybe the most fascinating method of travel was apparition. This magical method was all about The Three Ds: Destination, Determination, and Deliberation. A traveling witch or wizard had to be determined in the way they focused on their desired destination. They had to move with haste. And they had to disappear from their current location and instantly reappear at the desired location, but with deliberation. In other words, apparition was a form of teleportation, the imagined way of travel that uses tech to get you very quickly to where you want to go.

This speed and ease of travel came with its own set of problems. For one thing, apparition came with a noise, ranging from a quiet pop to a loud crack. And it could lead to injury, if botched. Even house-elves could apparate. But only skilled wizards and witches could apparate without a wand. Novice wizards with little experience could drop body parts when they practiced apparating. This happened when the wizard hadn't enough determination to reach their goal. Some body parts simply failed to arrive at the destination with the wizard. It must be quite annoying, leaving a leg behind.

The other magical travel method similar to teleportation was the use of Vanishing Cabinets. A pair of Vanishing Cabinets acted as a passageway between two places. An object placed in one cabinet would appear in the other. They were able to transport witches and wizards, too. For instance, they were very popular during the First Wizarding War. In those times, they were used to hide from Death Eater attacks. A wizard would disappear to the 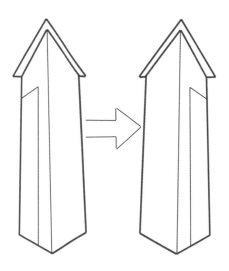 other cabinet until the peril had passed. But if one of the cabinets was broken, an object traveling between the two was trapped in a type of limbo.

So, getting about in the wizarding world was easy. But how possible will Muggle teleportation be in the future?

A Brief History of Fantasy Teleportation

Teleportation has been in Muggle fantasy tales for many years. Teleportation is the dream of being able to send matter across space, in an instant, and re-create it exactly, in another place. Many myths and magical tales have people being spirited away, as if by teleportation. But in these stories the travel is usually seen as being magical, or being some godly gift. The first example of modern teleportation by tech came in 1877. The story was called "The Man Without a Body," and it was written by Edward Page. In this short tale, the Muggle scientist, after discovering how to disassemble his cat, telegraphs its atoms and then reassembles them. Sadly, while he was trying to repeat the experiment on himself, an unlucky and badly timed power outage meant only his head was sent. Ouch.

This kind of teleportation problem seems common. In "The Fly," originally a 1957 short story but also made into three different movies, the horrible problems of teleportation are explored in detail. A Muggle scientist, testing teleportation, accidentally ends up fusing himself with a fly in what is meant to be horrific, but is in fact a very funny series of events. Perhaps it depends upon your sense of humor.

Over the years, teleportation has become common in Muggle fantasy tales. In the 1939 Buck Rogers serial, teleportation was the travel means of choice for moving characters from one place to another. When most older Muggles hear the word "teleportation," they at once think of the phrase "Beam me up, Scotty," from *Star Trek*. In this old but influential Muggle television series, they had at first planned to have characters land their spacecraft on planets. But they ran out of Muggle money. So the special-effects department came up with the creative idea of a transporter that could teleport characters down to the planet instead!

A Brief History of Muggle Teleportation

How would Muggle science teleport something from one place to another? Well, transporting matter like this would mean the original object or person would need to be destroyed! Then, they'd have to be pieced together in another place. You can see how this method might be a problem for Muggle scientists! What if the piecing together doesn't go according to plan? There are trillions of atoms in the human body. And that means a person would have to be broken down into individual atoms before each atom was noted, digitized, and teleported. Then the whole process would have to be done in reverse, to assemble them in the new place. And where would the Muggle soul go, assuming Muggles have souls, of course? (This also brings up the question of splitting the soul into many parts, as Voldemort did. We talk about this in the next chapter!)

One way of avoiding the teleportation problems is copies. In other words, you create a copy of the person or object you want to transport. So, rather than destroying and rebuilding a Muggle who wants to teleport, you simply create an exact copy at your destination. Imagine that! How would you know which one of you was you?! Who exactly is the "original"?

Muggle progress on teleportation has been slow, mostly because it's complicated and may well be impossible! But in 2002, Australian Muggle scientists successfully teleported a laser beam by copying a particle of light known as a photon and then re-creating it at another location. Muggle science teams in Germany and America then also teleported atoms of the elements calcium and beryllium using similar tech. Further progress occurred in Denmark in 2006. There, Muggle scientists teleported an object a few feet! Okay, it's not very far, but it's a start! You have to remember that the tiny object the Danish Muggles teleported was made of billions of atoms!

Maybe one day Muggles will be able to teleport things. Professor Michio Kaku of City University of New York believes it's possible. He thinks the tech to teleport a living Muggle elsewhere on earth, or even to outer space, could be possible by the end of the century. But then again, none of us will be around to check to see if he was right. Professor Kaku is known for being optimistic about things like Muggle time travel and invisibility and has made a study of fantasy tech that may one day come true.

Professor Kaku says, "You know the expression 'Beam me up, Scotty,' we used to laugh at it. We physicists used to laugh when someone talked about teleportation and invisibility, something like that, but we don't laugh anymore—we realized we were wrong on this one. Quantum teleportation already exists. At an atomic level we do it already. It's called quantum entanglement." What does Professor Kaku mean by this? He's talking about the fact that some Muggles think that matter has lots of hidden connections, and that might mean in the future that information can be sent in an almost magical way. "I think within a decade we will teleport the first molecule," Professor Kaku says.

WHAT IS THE MUGGLE VERSION OF THE HORCRUX?

"Well, you split your soul, you see, and hide part of it in an object outside the body. Then, even if one's body is attacked or destroyed, one cannot die, for part of the soul remains earthbound and undamaged. But of course, existence in such a form . . ."
—Professor Slughorn describes Horcruxes in J. K. Rowling, *Harry Potter and the Half-Blood Prince* (2005)

It was Voldemort's party piece. He split his soul and hid parts of it in objects outside his body. Then, even if his body was attacked or destroyed, he could not die, as part of his soul was saved—it stayed earthbound and unhurt. Horcrux is the word used for a magical object in which a person has hidden part of their soul in this way. And it's a way of cheating death.

To create a Horcrux, a witch or wizard had to commit calculated murder. The act of murder would hurt their soul. And that hurt could be used to cast a spell, which would rip off a hurt part of their soul and place it in an object. If the wizard or witch were later killed, they would cheat death, living on without a body. But there were also ways of collecting the pieces of split soul and putting them back into a body.

Voldemort "pushed his soul to the limit" in creating his seven Horcruxes. It made his soul weak, and likely to break apart if Voldemort was killed. The whole thing started when Voldemort created a Horcrux during his fifth year at Hogwarts. Wizard-kind usually thought of just a single Horcrux. But Voldemort made seven Horcruxes, maybe hoping that seven would make him stronger than just making one.

And, in the real world, Muggles have long dreamed of cheating death. In the past, most Muggle ideas about cheating death have been religious. But that science may also be able to someday move us beyond just our bodies. Cheating death may be just around the corner.

Cheating Death Through "Elec-trickery"

There's a very famous old story about cheating death. It's the Frankenstein story, written by Mary Shelley in 1818. This is how the story came about.

In June 1816, Mary and her soon-to-be husband, the famous English poet Percy Shelley, went to visit another famous English poet, Lord Byron. Lord Byron had a house at Lake Geneva, in Switzerland. It was a very weird time in history. 1816 was the "Year Without A Summer" because lots of the planet was caught in a volcanic winter. This winter had been triggered by the eruption of Mount Tambora the year before. Mary and the poets were kept indoors by the terrible weather, so they had long spooky chats about German ghost stories. They also talked about the way that electricity could make bodies shudder back into what looked like life. They decided each to write a perfect "ghost" story, and Mary's story became *Frankenstein: or, The Modern Prometheus.*

Frankenstein is really a tale about cheating death. The story's main character is a scientist called Victor Frankenstein. And Victor's dream is getting power through science, the kind of power that Muggles used to think only the gods should have. Victor starts to wonder about questions like: What is life? He uses electricity to make dead matter come back to life. He builds a grotesque creature using body parts from graveyards (yes, it's a very dark story indeed!).

Mary Shelley was caught up in the Muggle excitement about electricity at the time. All through Europe, Muggles were thrilled about the use of this new force of electricity, and how it might be used to create life or even cheat death. Some of Victor Frankenstein's speeches about the new science in the book make him sound like a wizard. "They ascend into the heavens: they have discovered how the blood circulates, and the nature of the air that we breathe. They have acquired new and almost unlimited powers; they can command the thunders of heaven, mimic the earthquake, and even mock the invisible world with its shadows."

Machine Horcrux

That first promise of electricity Muggles believed in never did come true. But, today, some Muggles think they can cheat death by using machines. The idea is that Muggle engineers will be able to upload Muggle consciousness to a machine. What do we mean by "consciousness"? Well, imagine someone's body no longer worked, but their mind was healthy. It might be possible to upload their memories, thoughts and experiences, everything that makes them who they are, into a machine like a computer. That won't be an easy thing to do, and it may be impossible! After all, a Muggle's consciousness would also include the way their brain works. And so that would also have to be put into the machine, in a similar way to placing part of Voldemort's soul in a Horcrux.

If your consciousness was put into a computer in this way, you might be able to cheat death. In some modern Muggle science fiction stories, consciousness is even put into another body, or maybe into a robot that looked human. Such robots are known as androids. Then you could move about in the Muggle world, but also think and act a thousand times faster than normal Muggles, as part of you would be robot brained! In fact, like Voldemort, why stop at one copy? If "you" could be uploaded in this way, why not upload yourself into seven different robot bodies, in the same way Voldemort created his seven Horcruxes?!

But, wait a moment. Is acting like Voldemort such a good idea? And what would it feel like to cheat death? Maybe a Frankenstein movie has the answer to this question. In the 1994 movie *Mary Shelley's Frankenstein*, the love of Victor Frankenstein's life is Elizabeth. When she is murdered, Victor tries to cheat her death by bringing her back to life. Then comes the strangely moving scene where we see Elizabeth's face when she understands what Victor has done. She is chilled by the unnatural and utterly horrific way in which she has cheated death. She goes quite mad at the monstrous state of limbo in which she finds herself. So, when you think about Voldemort's Horcruxes and this Frankenstein movie scene, maybe cheating death isn't such a good idea after all!

IS IT JUST WIZARDS AND WITCHES WHO WAVE WANDS?

"Wands are only as powerful as the wizards who use them.
Some wizards just like to boast that theirs are bigger and better
than other people's."
—J. K. Rowling, *Harry Potter and the Deathly Hallows* (2007)

Redwood, rosewood, rowan, or vine? Blackthorn, beech, or willow? Wand of what magical kind, lurks 'neath a wizard's pillow? In Harry's world, wand wood came in almost forty different flavors. And wand makers catered for a host of different cores. You could fill your wand with phoenix feather, dragon heartstring, unicorn hair, or thirteen other exotic options.

The wand was the witch's or wizard's weapon of choice. It was the object through which a wizard or witch wielded their magical powers. And that meant wands were vital to wizard-kind. Wands were of different lengths and flexibilities. But, more importantly, the wands were carefully made from the various woods, with the magical substance that ran through their core.

What happened when wood and core combined? It meant the wand had a kind of character and intelligence of its own. And the various wands that were made for witches and wizards were wide-ranging. In the magical world, most spells were done with wands. That's because wandless magic needed far more flair and skill. Wand magic was usually conjured up with an incantation. But wiser and more experienced wizards could also cast spells without speaking. And that meant the spell was hidden until cast, and could stop an opponent from protecting against it.

Every single wand was unique. Though wand cores may come from the same creature, and the wood from the same tree, no two wands were exactly alike. And, depending on the character of the wood and magical creature from which it came, wands were said to be "quasi-sentient." That means they held such a great deal of magic that they had an intelligence of their own (sentient means "able to experience feelings"). Wands were made and sold in Great Britain by the Ollivander family, who began wand manufacture in 382 BC.

The study of the history and the magical properties of wands was known as wandlore. Wandlore was a complex and mysterious branch of magic. It included the idea that a wand chose the wizard, and not the other way around, and that wands could switch allegiance. But is there a wandlore in Muggle history? Is it just witches and wizards who wave wands?

Wand as Symbol

These days it seems the wand is everywhere in the Muggle world, too. Wands have been famously wielded by make-believe Muggle characters, such as by Cinderella's godmother, by the mages and warlocks of the video game *World of Warcraft*, and by Gandalf in *The Hobbit*. Gandalf's name was invented by Tolkien, the author of *The Hobbit*, and it means "elf of the wand."

Muggle science has used the word "wand" for many inventions. Wand is the word for a handheld metal detector, such as those used at airports. Wand is also used to mean the steering wheel control stalks for lights, windshield wipers, and so on, in cars and other modern Muggle vehicles. And in Muggle music, the word "wand" is used for a conductor's baton, when he or she seems to conjure up music from the orchestra.

Muggles have also dabbled in "magic" wands over the centuries. Some Stone Age cave paintings show early Muggles holding wands, which may have been symbols of their power. And wands also appear in the artwork of the ancient Egyptians. Let's think about the fact that the Ollivander family have been making wands since 382 BC. Yes, of course it's fiction, but it's also maybe because Muggle cultures at the time were also making wands. One example is the Druid cultures that existed in Europe, before Christianity. The wizards, or sorcerers, of the Druid magical ceremonies would wield wands made of willow, yew, hawthorn, and other tree woods they thought were sacred. Such wands were only carved at dusk or dawn, as this was thought to be the best time to capture the sun's power. And the carving itself was carried out using a sacred knife, which had been dipped in blood. The wand was a symbol of power in Christianity, too. The Old Testament tale tells of Moses wielding a magic wand, in the form of a shepherd's staff, to both divide the Red Sea and to draw water out of a rock.

Like the Elder Wand, ancient Muggle "magic" wands are still with us. From Egypt and dating back to 2800 BC, these ancient wands are carved from hippopotamus ivory. As the hippopotamus is known as one of the most aggressive and dangerous creatures in Africa, any wizard that wielded a wand made from the beast would surely be able to tap into badass hippopotamus power!

The hippopotamus wasn't the only creature featured in ancient Egyptian wands. So-called apotropaic wands (apotropaic meaning "to prevent evil") were used to ward away the power of demons. Dating from around 2100 BC, they were curved and decorated with magical creatures such as the griffin and the sphinx, as well as more ordinary animals such as bulls and baboons, cats and crocodiles, panthers and lions (assuming you could catch them!), snakes and frogs.

The Most Mysterious Muggle Wand

Finally, the best-ever Muggle wand story comes from the oldest known ceremonial burial in Western Europe. It is the year 1823. A lone Muggle horseman gallops through the night, decked out in tall top hat and flowing gown. His destination: the southwest coast of the land of Merlin: Wales, and, in particular, the Gower peninsula. The horseman rides into history, into the Muggle past. Into all our pasts.

The Muggle on the horse is one of a new breed of detectives. He is Professor William Buckland, "master of rocks," or professor of geology, at Oxford University. And he's armed with a hammer. Our professor is about to make an earth-shattering discovery. He was called to Paviland cave, one of the caves in the Gower's limestone rocks. The cave had first been found the year before, but now in 1823, one of the Muggle world's most important finds was about to be unearthed. For what Buckland was about to discover would help unravel the story of Muggle history itself.

In that dark cave, Buckland found the first Muggle human fossil recovered anywhere in the world. But that's not all. In Buckland's words:

I found the skeleton enveloped by a coating of a kind of ochre . . . which stained the earth, and in some parts extended itself to the distance of about half an inch around the surface of the bones. . . . Close to that part of the thigh bone where the pocket is usually worn surrounded also by ochre [were] about two handfuls of the Nerita littoralis [periwinkle shells]. At another part of the skeleton, viz. in contact with the ribs [were] forty or fifty fragments of ivory wands [also] some small fragments of rings made of the same ivory and found with the wands. . . . Both wands and rings, as well as the Nerite shells, were stained superficially with red, and lay in the same red substance that enveloped the bones.

Buckland had also found a mammoth skull lying along with the bones. The professor's diagnosis was typical of his time. As a creationist, Buckland misjudged both the skeleton's age and its sex. For our professor believed no Muggle remains could have been older than the Great Flood in the Bible. So he got the age wrong. He thought the remains were female, mostly because he found jewelry, including a wand. The wand was thought to be elephant ivory, but is now known to be carved from the tusk of a mammoth.

So Buckland thought the mammoth wand and other remains belonged to a witch. Perhaps the old Welsh witch was based at a nearby Roman camp. But, Buckland felt, it was definitely a woman. Just look at the evidence. There was the wand. There was the jewelry. And there were the remains, covered with red ochre. In fact, thanks to Buckland, the human remains are still known to this day as the Red Lady of Paviland. And yet, this was no ordinary Muggle skeleton.

Now begins a remarkable journey during which this wanded skeleton changes the very idea of Muggle time. Over the years, since the discovery in 1823, Muggle scholars have found out some amazing things about the Red Lady. Firstly, he wasn't a lady. He was a man. And a young man, at that. He was no older than his twenties. Because his skeleton was found without a skull, Muggle scholars found it hard to judge his height. But he may have been about 5 feet, 8 inches tall and around 150 pounds in weight. The missing skull also sadly stopped the scholars from reconstructing his face. Headless burials were common in Europe in Stone Age times. Though it could also be that the man's skull washed away when the cave was flooded. Whatever the reason, the face of this man, this wizard of the Stone Age, one of the most ancient of British ancestors, will remain a mystery.

The Most Ancient Wizard

The professor could never have imagined the real story of the Muggle remains found in that cave. The skeleton he called a witch was, at the time of the discovery, the first modern Muggle skeleton to be found anywhere in the world. And it remains the oldest ever found in the UK, as well as the oldest ritual burial found in Western Europe. When Muggles did their math on the remains in 2009, they decided the bones were 33,000 years old.

There have been further finds in the area where the "Red Lady" was discovered. Thousands of flints, teeth, and bones, as well as needles and bracelets, have been found. All this evidence means that the cave was visited regularly by our Muggle ancestors for around 10,000 years, until the last ice age would have forced them to head south.

So the "Red Lady" is in fact evidence of one of the oldest known wizards. It's likely the cave was sacred to Stone Age peoples. Magicians may have contacted the spirit world from the cave. And all this, as well as the mammoth's skull found with the skeleton, have convinced Muggles that the Red Lady was himself a "wizard," or at least an important tribal chieftain. Who knows, this famous wanded skeleton may even have been the Dumbledore of his day.